**Anatomy
of the
Ship**

The 20-gun ship
BLANDFORD

**Anatomy
of the
Ship**

The 20-gun ship

BLANDFORD

Peter Goodwin

Naval
Institute
Press

Frontispiece
1. Model of a 20-gun Sixth Rate *c*1719,
built to the 1719 Establishment. It could be
either the *Blandford* or *Lyme*, as both were
built to the same draught. The model
conforms very closely to the original plans
with a few small differences, for instance the
ballast port and the aftermost sweep port are
both positioned a little further forward than
shown on the draught. It clearly shows the
sweeps and is fitted out with eleven swivel
guns each side, which suggests that it was
built to show all the possible features of a
20-gun ship of this period.
National Maritime Museum

© Peter Goodwin 1988

First published in Great Britain 1988 by
Conway Maritime Press Ltd
24 Bride Lane, Fleet Street,
London EC4Y 8DR

Published and distributed in the United
States of America and Canada by the
Naval Institute Press, Annapolis,
Maryland 21402.

Library of Congress Catalog Card No.
87−63031

ISBN 0−87021−058−0

Contents

FOREWORD AND ACKNOWLEDGEMENTS

At the end of the eighteenth century the naval frigate proved to be a great asset to the fleet for conveying dispatches and messages and for monitoring the movements of enemy fleets. They originated from much simpler craft which had been developed from what were known as galley-frigates and the 20-gun ships of the 1719 Establishment. A model of this type of 20-gun ship at the Science Museum in South Kensington has intrigued me ever since I first saw it at an early age so it seems only fitting to have researched and compiled a work covering such ships, which to some extent have been neglected in favour of the larger vessels of the British fleet such as 100- and 74-gun ships.

I would not have been able to complete this work without those who assisted me in the search for suitable plans, models and various other sources. I must firstly thank David White and the staff of the Draught Room at the National Maritime Museum for the plans, and discussions concerning the more unusual aspects of construction of this period. Secondly I would like to thank two other staff at the National Maritime Museum: David Lyon who pursued sources covering the armament, and David Tull for a visit to the models kept at Kidbrooke. A special thanks must be given to David Sambrooke for kindly lending me photographs to work from, which provided the detail necessary for such a book as this. Also my thanks go to James Lees who sorted out problems concerning a detailed aspect of the rigging and sails. A final acknowledgement is extended to the staff of the Public Records Office at Kew and to all the others at the National Maritime Museum who helped.

Peter Goodwin 1987

Introduction

THE DEVELOPMENT OF THE 20-GUN SHIP

The role of the 20-gun Sixth Rate in the Royal Navy during the early part of the eighteenth century is somewhat overshadowed by the great fleet actions of the period. However, although the names of these small vessels do not often come to the notice of history, their presence was essential to the integrity of the fleet and the wellbeing of merchant shipping. These ships carried out the rather mundane tasks of convoy escort to merchant ships, of dispatch vessels, fleet scouts and fire-support for amphibious assaults.

The general layout of the *Blandford* type, with a row of oarports below the gundeck, can be traced back to the early seventeenth century. The National Maritime Museum at Greenwich holds a drawing of a vessel of 96 feet on the keel, 32 feet breadth and 12 feet draught (368 tons) that has been dated to about 1625. Evidence suggests that no ship was built to this plan, but the galley-frigate arrangement with a separate rowing deck is evident.

Sweeps (or long oars) were widely used by small warships and merchantmen in the seventeenth century – probably only for slow speed manoeuvring – but it was to be half a century before the Royal Navy introduced a genuine galley-frigate. This was inspired by the activities of the Barbary pirates, who employed the classic Mediterranean-type galley in attacks on merchant shipping. They galleys were armed with heavy forward-firing guns and consequently attacked head-on, offering only a narrow, and low, target. Depending largely on their oars, they could outmanoeuvre square-rigged sailing ships in most weather conditions, allowing the galleys to attack the vulnerable bow or stern, where few guns could be brought to bear.

Clearly a new type of warship was called for to counter this menace, and the result was the *Charles Galley* and the *James Galley* of 1676, supposedly inspired by the French 24-gun *La Bien-Aimée*, built at Toulon in 1672. The *Charles* was designed by Anthony Deane Jnr, and built by Phineas Pett III at Woolwich. She had a lower deck length of 134 feet, moulded breadth of 28 feet 6 inches and a depth in the hold of 8 feet 7 inches, measuring 492 tons. Armed with 6 sakers (later 6-pounders) on the lower deck, 22 sakers on the gundeck and four 3-pounders, the *Charles Galley* was designated a Fourth Rate. The *James Galley*, built at Blackwall by Anthony Deane Jnr, was slightly smaller, but used the same general proportions and mounted 30 guns.

Both vessels were regarded as a success under both sail and oars, but were less satisfactory as warships, since they were very large for their armament. A further very similar vessel, the *Mary Galley* was built in 1687, but the type received major official recognition after the 1688 Revolution, when the new Admiralty regime ordered a series of smaller but similar vessels, beginning with the *Experiment* of 1689. Originally intended to have a lower deck fitted for oars only, they eventually acquired a few gunports on that level, becoming what the French termed *demi-batterie* ships. They varied in detail from ship to ship but were about 106 feet on the gundeck, 27½ feet in breadth and about 380 tons, and were armed with 32 to 36 guns.

Their loss rate in the ensuing French wars was very high (about 30 per cent of the whole class was lost to the enemy, and a number more to stress of weather) which suggested that they were at the same time not powerful enough for the job but too small for their armament. A few more were built after 1706 to slightly enlarged dimensions but thereafter the type was superseded by larger two-decker 40-gun ships and smaller single-decker Sixth Rates of 20 or 24 guns.

At this time the term 'galley' was applied to any vessel which could employ oars, even in an auxiliary role, which is attested to by the large number of vessels with the suffix *Galley* in their names. This applied to many of the swifter merchant ships of the period, which may have employed their oars on the 'tween deck, like a naval galley-frigate. This was certainly true of Captain William Kidd's notorious *Adventure Galley* built in 1695. Even single-decked vessels, like the 20-gun *Peregrine Galley* of 1700, acquired this sobriquet if they operated oars from ports between the guns on the upper deck. The *Peregrine*, which proved a remarkably good sailer, was a 'freelance' design by the Marquis of Carmarthen, whose enthusiasm for oars eventually over-reached itself – he persuaded the Admiralty to build a 40-gun ship, the *Anne Galley*, with two rows of oar ports: it was an expensive failure.

After 1706 Sixth Rates were single-decked, but in 1718 a return was made to the original concept of the galley-frigates of 1689 for a vessel called the *Dursley Galley*. This ship had no gunports (only oarports) on the lower deck, reducing the armament to twenty 6-pounders, but keeping the 1689 dimensions, which produced a better balanced design.

In 1719 an enquiry was convened to try to produce improvements in ship design and construction. The committee, led by the Surveyor of the Navy, Sir Jacob Acworth, consisted of the master shipwrights of the royal dockyards and reported to the Admiralty in November. Possibly in response to the additional firepower called for in the 1716 Gun Establishment, the recommendations generally involved an increase in dimensions, and were formalised as the 1719 Establishment. The new dimensions were intended to ensure that all ships 'may now properly be built so as to prove good sailers as well as ships of force . . . making the said ships stronger and lighter but also cause them to be built cheaper and better sea boats.' In specific terms for the Sixth Rates this meant taking the best available model: 'The 20-gun ships are conformed to the *Dursley Galley*, which works and sails well.' Thus, there was a return in effect to a thirty-year-old design but with the armament reduced to a more reasonable scale.

Although later enlarged the essential layout of the 20-gun ships remained unaltered until after 1745 when they were superseded by true 'frigate-built' vessels (*ie* with a complete unarmed lower deck set at or below the waterline, producing a lower, more stable, and more seaworthy ship). As originally built, the 1719 20s of the *Blandford* type were probably quite effective, but the history of the 1689 ships repeated itself, with the 20s gradually acquiring lower

TABLE 1: 20-GUN SIXTH RATES BUILT OR CONVERTED ACCORDING TO THE 1719 ESTABLISHMENT

Name	Launched	Dockyard	Shipwright	Origin	Fate
Blandford	13.2.1720	Deptford	Stacey	New building	Sold for £228, 1739
Greyhound	13.2.1720	Deptford	Stacey	New building	Paid off 1732; broken up 1741
Shoreham	25.8.1720	Woolwich	Hayward	Rebuild of 32-gun ship of 1694	Bomb vessel 1727; sold 1744
Lyme	8.11.1720	Deptford	Stacey	Rebuild of 32-gun ship of 1694	Broken up 1738
Scarborough	19.7.1722	Deptford	Stacey	Rebuild of 32-gun ship of 1711	Sold for £225, 1739
Lowestoffe	18.12.1723	Portsmouth	Naish	Rebuilt of 32-gun ship of 1697	Paid off 1733; sold 1744
Garland	1.5.1734	Sheerness	Ward	New building	Sold for £1003, 1744
Rose	8.9.1724	Woolwich	Hayward	Rebuild of 20-gun ship of 1712	Hulked 1739; sold 1744
Seaford	22.10.1724	Deptford	Stacey	Rebuild of 24-gun ship of 1697	Bomb vessel 1727; broken up 1740
Deal Castle	6.4.1727	Sheerness	Ward	Rebuild of 24-gun ship of 1706	Sold for £191, 1746
Gibraltar	8.8.1727	Deptford	Stacey	Rebuild of 20-gun ship of 1711	Sold for £340, 1748
Bideford	2.10.1727	Chatham	Rosewell	Rebuild of 24-gun ship of 1711	Lost off Flamborough Head, 1737
Seahorse	7.10.1727	Deptford	Stacey	Rebuild of 20-gun ship of 1712	Sold for £245, 1748
Squirrel	19.10.1727	Woolwich	Hayward	Rebuild of 24-gun ship of 1707	Sold for £260, 1749
Rye	21.10.1727	Chatham	Rosewell	New building	Broken up 1735
Aldborough	21.10.1727	Portsmouth	Allin	Rebuild of 20-gun ship of 1705	Broken up, 1742
Flamborough	21.10.1727	Portsmouth	Allin	Rebuild of 24-gun ship of 1707	Sold for £331, 1749
Experiment	1.11.1727	Plymouth	Lock	Rebuild of a 32-gun ship of 1689	Broken up 1738
Fox	18.11.1727	Deptford	Stacey	Rebuild of 24-gun ship of 1702	Broken up 1736
Phoenix	16.1.1728	Woolwich	Hayward	Rebuild of 24-gun ship of 1709	Sold for £201, 1744
Sheerness	4.1.1732	Deptford	Stacey	New building	Sold for £240, 1744
Dolphin	6.1.1732	Deptford	Stacey	New building	Fireship 1747; captured 1760

deck gunports, and more substantial upperworks in the form of longer forecastles and quarterdecks, higher rails, and so forth.

Part of the reason for this may lie with the early eighteenth century policy of 'rebuilding', a term which had a myriad of meanings. On the one hand it might simply mean a major reconstruction, but on the other hand there were cases of ships taken to pieces and rebuilt to very different designs, occasionally retaining little more than the name of the original vessel. A number of *Blandford*'s nominal sister ships were actually rebuilt from the earlier 32-gun *demi-batterie* Fifth Rates, which had some gunports on the lower deck. This may have influenced the rebuilding, and there is certainly evidence that the 20-gun ships departed more from the Establishment details than ships of higher rates. The Establishment itself was modified in 1733, 1741 and 1745 and thereafter 20-gun ships officially carried two gunports a side aft of a midships ballast port on the lower deck, and were re-rated as 24s. Being relatively cheap the Sixth Rates may have been the subject of much *ad hoc* experimentation, and the large number of 'non-standard' models which do not agree with draughts provides strong evidence of this.

Detailed developments included a retrograde move from the round bow to the beakhead bulkhead (when the forecastle became more substantial) and an elaboration of the after cabin to include full quarter galleries in lieu of the quarter badges carried by the earlier ships. Combined with the higher and more substantial upperwork, these changes gradually reduced the stability and seaworthiness of the Sixth Rates to a point in the late 1740s where they were finally condemned as totally unsuitable cruising ships. The Anson administration ordered the first true frigates in 1747 as 24s (the *Unicorn* and *Lyme*, which were soon rerated as 28s) as direct successors to these inadequate vessels, and thereafter the frigate principle was applied to larger (32- and 36-gun ships) and smaller (20-gun) cruising ships.

THE BLANDFORD'S HISTORY

The *Blandford* was built to replace a previous ship bearing the same name which, while under the command of Captain Erasmus Phillips, was 'lost in the Bay' (of Biscay) on 28 March 1718/19. The new ship was constructed under the supervision of Richard Stacey, Master Shipwright of Deptford. The official launching took place on Saturday 13 February 1719/20, but due to a number of problems she did not actually 'come off the dock' until 23 February. The initial cost of the hull was £3041 11s 3d amounting to a final sum of £3521 11s 3¾d after her overall fitting out.

The following calendar of events shows the considerable work carried out between her launching and the time she sailed for the Nore to join the Fleet on 12 March 1720

Wednesday 24 February: Gangs of shipwrights and joiners went aboard to complete the minor work, internal fittings and cabin bulkheads etc.

25 February – 27 February: Spent shipping and setting up the masts, yards and rigging. (This appears to have been a formidable achievement especially when one considers that the hours of daylight at this period of the year were very short.)

28 February: Loaded with ballast, generally in the form of shingle. This was used to lower the centre of gravity to counter-balance the topweight of the masts and yards etc above.

Monday 29 February (leap year): Anchor cables loaded.

1 March 1720: Sails bent onto the yards.

2 March: Anchors and additional ballast embarked.

3 March: Moved from the sheer hulk (used for shipping the masts) to the gallows (crane) where she spent the following seven days embarking her twenty 6-pounder carriage guns, boatswain's and carpenter's stores, and carried out her victualling.

11 March: Loaded with powder and shot

A week later she left British waters on an assignment to Copenhagen,

TABLE 2: ESTIMATED COSTS

COSTS FOR A 24-GUN and 20-GUN SHIP

	24 guns	20 guns
Hull	£2703	£2503
Masts and Yards	£97	£97
Rigging, fitted	£180	£180
Eight months' boatswains' and carpenters' stores	£930	£930
	£3910	£3710

COSTS FOR A 20-GUN SHIP

Figurehead 'Lyon'	£6	10s	0d
Trailboard, both sides	£1	3s	6d
Tafferal	£9	0s	0d
Quarter pieces, both	£6	0s	0d
	£22	13s	6d

COSTS OF FIGUREHEAD AND ORNAMENTATION, c1745

Lion	£7	4s	0d
Trailboards	£1	4s	0d
Tafferal	£9	8s	0d
Quarter pieces	£10	0s	0d
	£27	16s	0d

arriving on Wednesday 6 May 1720, where she remained until her final return to the Nore on 2 December.

The following year her duties took her further afield, sailing for South Carolina on 9 February 1720/21 from Deptford. Ten days later on 19 February her fore mast sprung during heavy weather. Two days later when the weather had improved, the mast was 'fished' with two halves of an anchor stock, a temporary arrangement that had to suffice until she reached her destination.

The *Blandford* arrived off Charleston, South Carolina on 9 June 1721. Two days later an entry was made in the Master's log referring to the condition of the provisions: 'Survey of our Bread and Cast 1156 Pounds Rotten, not fit for a man to eat and saw it over Board by Order'. (This is a powerful reminder that foodstuffs deteriorated rapidly within the dank confines of the ship's hold.)

Whilst on station at Charleston, *Blandford* was employed in the escort duties that many of the small vessels like her were designed for, and on Friday 14 June sailed with the 20-gun *Flamborough* with a small convoy of merchantmen. Between 22 September and 7 November the ship was laid up in Quelcher Creek and underwent minor repairs. It was during this period that her damaged fore mast was replaced with a new mast and the opportunity was taken to careen and pay the underwater hull. The remaining two years on foreign station saw the ship running between Charleston and the West Indies carrying out escort and dispatch duties. *Blandford* finally sailed for England on 6 August 1724 and on arrival she underwent a refit at Portsmouth.

For the next six years *Blandford* remained in home waters plying between Plymouth and the Nore with the exception of a brief period where she was sent to Gibraltar. She sailed on 16 July 1727 and as before when leaving British waters ran into bad luck, for on her first day out from Spithead she lost both her main and mizzen topmasts. She finally reached the 'Rock' on 28 July to join the squadron under Sir Charles Wager. The squadron consisted of the *Torbay* 80, *Stirling Castle* 70, nine other warships, the *Success* (store ship), the bomb *Thunder* and the sloop *Hawk*. During the whole of this period the ship

underwent a number of refits and annual dockings for re-paying the underwater hull, both at Portsmouth and Sheerness.

In 1730 the *Blandford* was once again sent back to the American Colonies working between Charleston and Boston carrying out escort duties. She remained on this station until her recall to England in 1732.

One aspect that does come to light during the period prior to 1732 is that which concerns modifications made to her structure. An entry made in the Master's log for 25 May 1731 states: 'Hauled ashore to the Wharf in order to drive and clench the Bolts of the Ryders on the Larboard side'. This statement poses the question of whether the riders (internal frames) were built into the ship when she was originally constructed or fitted later during a refit. Riders were fitted in the midship section of the hold to give additional strength to the hull, but the 1719 Establishment makes no reference to riders being fitted to 20-gun ships so it could be assumed that there was no need for them on this size of vessel. However, two alternative answers can be given: one being that they were fitted on initial building at the discretion and experience of the builder; or that they were later fitted to strengthen the ship, thereby increasing her lifespan or to overcome any shortcomings in the construction and design. It was considered normal practice during the eighteenth century to install floor and futtock riders and toptimber riders to prolong a ship's life, and as this was the case it can be assumed that the riders were fitted during her refit at Sheerness in March 1727/28.

After her deployment in the American Colonies she returned to England and paid off at Sheerness on 25 July 1732. At this dockyard she underwent an extensive refit where a number of modifications were made to the quarter galleries, quarterdeck and forecastle. She was also fitted out with an iron firehearth with two copper kettles, an improvement that was to become common throughout the fleet. The overall expenditure for the work carried out was £1872 9s 9d, which was more than half her original building cost.

On completion of the refit she resumed her duties in home waters until 1738. Throughout this period she was docked once at Woolwich and five times at Portsmouth. Her docking at Woolwich in 1734 must have included considerable work and repairs, for the total cost came to £1799 6s 8d. It will appear from this that the overall condition of the ship was deteriorating quite rapidly for she had undergone a major refit only eighteen months earlier. However, this was quite common throughout the eighteenth century when the life of a wooden hull could only be extended at considerable cost.

Her final years were spent with the squadron under the command of Vernon, based at Port Royal, Jamaica. Here she carried out routine patrol work seeking out privateers and acting as escort to merchant convoys. This was a period of unrest, for Spain insisted that she had a trade monopoly in this area which caused much friction between the Spanish and the English, and was shortly to flare into the War of Jenkins' Ear.

In late January 1739/40 Vernon's squadron was heavily buffeted by gales when cruising off Cartagena, the squadron dispersed and ran for shelter at Port Royal. During this storm the *Blandford* yet again lost her fore mast and damaged her bowsprit and was kept in harbour for a while due to the lack of spare masts. This seems to have been quite a frequent problem for the vessels on this station, but so too was the lack of stores. Finally she sailed on 1 September escorting a convoy back to England, to return home for the last time.

By now the ship was, by eighteenth century standards, old and unfit for service and the following year she was surveyed and ordered to be sold. The Navy Board then ordered a new ship to be 'built in her room'. The last entry

made in the Captain's log reads as follows:

Saturday, 13 December 1741

These twenty four hours moderate and cloudy with small rain. This day the Admiralty ordered the Ships Company to three weeks liberty. Ditto said [three illegible words] Boatswain, the Lieutenant and the Master with some of the People impressing men in London. His Majestys ship *Blandford* condemned as unserviceable, Admiralty Order 15th January 1740/41. Was Discharged from and turned over into the Dover with the Whole Ships Company.

George Burrish

The ship was sold at Deptford on the 28 October 1742 for the sum of £222. Her successor, the new *Blandford*, was lost to the French in January 1745 while under the command of Captain Edward Dodd.

CONSTRUCTION

The *Blandford* was built to the specifications authorised by the 1719 Establishment. The Establishment List gave a complete inventory of the dimensions for all of the components required for the ship's construction. Also included were the more minor details such as bolt sizes, scarph lengths and general instructions governing standards and practices. These instructions, however, were only a guide (albeit a firm one) to the constructor, who in reality would use his discretion to interpret the requirement of the Navy Board. This does not imply that he would have deviated greatly from the rules, but would apply a more practical approach in order, for example, to reduce timber wastage. If a timber such as a carling were made half an inch less in scantling in order to use an existing stock the resulting deviation would have had little impact on the overall construction.

First the keel was laid. This was made from elm, chosen because it was durable when immersed in water for long periods and could receive a considerable number of bolts and nails without splitting. The keel was actually made in four lengths, each section being scarphed and bolted together. The sides of the keel were rabbeted throughout its length to receive the lower edge of the garboard strake, the lowest line of planking.

Rising vertically at the after end of the keel was the stern (or main) post. This was generally made from a single baulk of oak forming the after boundary of the vessel. In some cases, if a suitable piece of timber could not be obtained, a false post was fayed and bolted to the after side of the stern post to increase the overall scantling. It was either fitted fore or aft (according to the 1719 Establishment, aft). Supporting the structure forward of the stern post was the inner post and the deadwood, the latter consisting of a series of timbers that were scarphed together to form a large knee.

At the fore end of the keel was the stem post, a curved timber made up of pieces of 'compass oak' scarphed and bolted together. The stem post was further stiffened by the apron or false stem which was fayed to the after side. The stem post was joined to the keel by an intricate scarph called the 'boxing'. The lower part of the apron was continued aft into the fore deadwood, on to which the ship's frames were set and bolted through to the keel. This course of timber was in reality a continuation of the deadwood fitted fore and aft, the height diminishing towards the midship section of the ship, to comply with the height of the framing.

There does appear to be a number of peculiarities in the design of the *Blandford* and her sisters which show some departures from the accepted practice of warship construction at that time. Firstly there is the manner of the

TABLE 3: **BLANDFORD'S REFIT HISTORY**

Sixth Rate of 20 guns
Built at Deptford
Surveyor: Richard Stacey
Launched 13 February 1719/20

Initial hull costs	£3041	11s 3d
Cost of fitting out	£480	0s 8¾d
Final costs	£3521	11s 11¾d

Dimensions:	Length on the lower deck	106ft	0ins
	Length of the keel for tonnage	87ft	3ins
	Extreme breadth	26ft	5½ins
	Depth in the hold	9ft	2ins
	Burden	375, 18/94 tons	

Start date	Comp. date	Dockyard	Cost	Work done
5.12.1724	6.1.1724/25	Portsmouth	£501 1s 0d	General refit/careening
23.6.1727	28.6.1727	Portsmouth	£671 13s 2d	General refit
6.10.1727	13.10.1727	Portsmouth		General/sheathing
6.3.1727/28	26.3.1727/28	Sheerness		Major refit
20.8.1728	27.8.1728	Sheerness	£439 1s 8d	Careening/caulking
4.4.1729	5.4.1729	Sheerness	£148 16s 9d	Minor repear work
27.10.1729	26.11.1729	Portsmouth	£408 2s 10d	General refit/sheathing
25.7.1732	Arr. off Sheerness and payed off			
13.12.1732	3.2.1732/33	Sheerness	£1872 9s 9d	Extensive refit/repair
				Fitting of an iron firehearth with 2 copper kettles
			(Estimated cost of firehearth, £135 12s 0d)	
7.11.1733	5.12.1733	Portsmouth	£701 13s 6d	General/careening
14.11.1734	26.3.1734/35	Woolwich	£1799 6s 8d	Major refit
5.9.1735	2.10.1735	Portsmouth	£740 10s 8d	General refit
17.6.1736	5.7.1736	Portsmouth	£591 9s 6d	General refit
13.6.1737	30.7.1737	Portsmouth	£879 18s 7d	General refit/careening
20.2.1737/38	30.3.1737/38	Portsmouth	£480 8s 0d	General refit/sheathing for foreign service
1741	Surveyed to be sold, orders arranged to have a new ship built			
15.1.1740/41	Admiralty Order stating that she was to be sold			
13.12.1741	Captain and ships' company discharged from the ship and transferred to the *Dover*			
28.10.1742	Sold at Deptford for £222 0s 0d			

actual construction of the frames. Secondly there is the disposition of the framing in comparison with the 'room and space' regulation stipulated for the 20-gun ship.

Regarding the frame construction it can be seen that the *Blandford* was built with a square tuck stern (despite the fact that the square tuck had been abolished on most English men-of-war since about 1645), and also had a distinguishable long run forward for the dead flat. From these two features it can be assumed that the ship was built with square framing throughout the hull. Since about 1715 it had been accepted practice to fit cant frames in the extreme fore and after bodies of a ship. This form of construction was introduced to reduce the amount of timber wastage where the curvature of the hull towards the centre line became more pronounced, but it suited neither the requirements of the square tuck nor the very bluff bow formed by the length of the dead flat forward. However, quite a number of 20-gun ships were 'rebuilt' from 32-gun ships built during the first decade of the eighteenth century, all of which would have been built with square frames.

This period of naval construction can be classified as one of transition, when

old practices were applied alongside the new. It was to be another thirty years before frames were included on a set of draughts and even then it was rare. Thus it can be assumed that in most cases the individual builder would interpret the ships' drawings and specifications according to his own practices and experience.

The disposition of the framing also points to this period being one of transition. Unlike the later practice where every other frame position was marked on the draught, only every third frame is marked on those of the *Blandford* and other vessels in the same era. The overall distance between these frames was 7 feet 3 inches, which when divided by three gives a 'room and space' of 2 feet 5 inches which corresponds to the 20-gun ship dimension set down in the 1719 Establishment.

The fore and aft siding of each floor was 9 inches and each first futtock, $8\frac{1}{2}$ inches, giving a total 'room' of $17\frac{1}{2}$ inches. The remaining 'space' of $11\frac{1}{2}$ inches between each main or full frame permitted only one filling frame to be fitted. It was common practice to have two filling frames between each main frame, so it appears that this was a transitional system of framing. It can be assumed that the structure of each filling frame was made in the reverse fashion to its counterpart, in other words one was made up of a floor and second futtock, the next of a first and third futtock, and so on.

The main frames were made up in two 'slices' one half being made up of a floor, second futtock and toptimber, the other half, a first futtock, third futtock and toptimber, lengthening pieces being added to either as necessary. Sixth Rate ships of this period were not fitted with fourth futtocks but it can be assumed that some builders may have included them in order to reduce timber wastage or when suitable 'compass' oak could not be procured. When each component had been assembled to form each half of the full frame, the two halves were fayed and bolted together at the 'joint line'. This always corresponded to the divisions of the 'room and space' shown on the draught, in other words every 2 feet 5 inches.

The aftermost square frame formed the boundary of the square tuck transom, the frame terminating at its head below the wing transom. The space at the fore end of the ship forward of the foremost square frame (R) was filled in with the hawse pieces, so called because the hawse holes were cut through them.

Once all the frames or timbers had been set up in position the whole structure was made rigid by a series of longitudinal members. The first and most important of these was the keelson which ran fore and aft along the centre line directly above the keel. Towards the fore end the keelson continued up the after face of the apron, at which point it was generally referred to as the stemson. At the after end the keelson was married into a large knee called the sternson which gave additional support to the stern post.

Next to be wrought was what was generally known as the 'thick stuff'. This comprised a series of bands of heavy planking laid over the inner faces of the frames or timbers. The position at which each strake was laid corresponded to the joint lines of the floors and various futtocks. In a similar fashion the deck clamps were wrought at their respective deck levels, their function being to support the ends of the beams. The beams were fitted prior to the completion of both the internal and external planking.

The deck beams greatly enhanced the strength of the ship in its transverse plane. Most of the beams fitted in the midship section were fashioned from two lengths of pitch pine scarphed and bolted together, those fitted afore and abaft being short enough to be made out of a single timber. The beams were supported at their outboard ends by wooden brackets called knees, these being categorised as either hanging knees or lodging knees. The timber from which they were made was carefully selected or even grown to shape to ensure that the grain curvature gave the maximum strength required. The hanging knees were set vertically with the athwart arm bolted to the side of the beam and the perpendicular arm to the ship's side. The lodging knees were set in the horizontal plane with one arm bolted to the beam and the other to the side of the ship, its heel butting against the adjacent hanging knee on the next beam. Towards the fore and after end of the ship the hanging knees of the lower deck were inverted due to the diminishing shape of the hull; these were often referred to as standards. The beams of the fore and after platforms were not supported by hanging or lodging knees. The ends of these beams were simply shaped to fit and bolted down.

Worked intercostally between the beams were a series of lighter timbers called carlings and ledges. The carlings were laid longitudinally in two tiers, the innermost forming the boundaries of the hatchways and so on. The ledges were worked transversely between the tiers of carlings, usually three between each deck beam. Both carlings and ledges were only fitted on the upper and lower decks, with the exception of the companionway on the quarterdeck and where necessary on the platforms to support the galley firehearth.

The bottom planking was between 2 and 3 inches thick, the thicker boards forming the diminishing strakes below the main wale. Due to the complex hull shape at the fore and after ends, stealer and drop strakes were worked to prevent the boards 'snying'. The ends of the planks which were set into the rabbets of the stem and stern posts were called hood ends.

At this time the main wale was wrought in two strakes, 4 inches thick and 10 inches deep, with a filling strake wrought between them. The planking of the main wale was joined together by a 'hook and butt' scarph, the 'top and butt' and 'anchor stock' type being introduced later. The function of this heavily built wale was to bind the hull longitudinally to resist the 'hogging' and 'sagging' strains which afflicted wooden ships of this era. The rest of the ship's side was planked up with 2-inch boards.

Internally, waterways were worked along the side of the ship over the outboard ends of the beams. These strakes were fashioned to form a watertight seal between the deck and the ship's side. Above each waterway was a thick band of planking which was worked up to the level of either the sweep port or gunport sills on the lower and upper deck respectively. This band of planking was called the spirketting and it served the same purpose as that of the main wale. The spirketting was usually wrought in the 'top and butt' fashion. The space between the spirketting and the deck clamps was worked up with relatively thin planking known as the lining or 'quickwork'.

Adjacent to the keelson was a longitudinal known as the limberstrake which acted as a clamp to hold the floor timbers. The remaining lining which covered the floors of the hold was known as the footwaling.

The framing of the stern comprised a series of counter timbers which were set up and bolted at their heels to the wing transom which supported the whole of the stern structure above the stern post. The counter timbers were braced laterally with deck transoms and transom beams, and planked up with 2-inch boards. At the fore part of the hull the structure was stiffened with deck hooks and breast hooks which were wrought across the inboard side of the hawse pieces.

DECORATION

This description of the Blandford's decoration is speculative, for no sources relating specifically to her decoration design appear to exist. The following

information has been compiled by careful examination of a number of existing contemporary models and by assessment of their general recurring features. The degree of decoration and carved work on *Blandford* was, by comparison to that of seventeenth century vessels, somewhat modest. Much of the carved work which was to be found on these earlier ships had been reduced due to the restrictions imposed by the Navy Board Order of 1703. This was promulgated both to reduce the unnecessary expenses incurred in the decoration of ships and to minimise the amount of good timber being wasted on superfluous adornment.

The majority of decoration was restricted to the head and stern of the ship. The main feature at the head of the ship was the figurehead which in *Blandford*'s case probably consisted of the heraldic rampant 'Lyon' wearing the royal crown. (It is worth noting that the two models representing 20-gun ships of this period which are in the Henry Huddleston Rogers Collection at the Naval Academy in Annapolis have individual figureheads in place of the more common lion form.) This form of figurehead was common to all vessels with the exception of First and Second Rates which bore individual figures. It was to be another eight years before this privilege was extended to the lesser rates (by the Navy Board Order of 1727), and even then it was quite a number of years before the practice became general in the smallest rates of men-of-war.

The figurehead was supported by a number of head rails leading aft in a serpentine curve to the ship's side adjacent to the catheads. Each of these rails was fashioned with an individual moulding. The head rails were supported by vertical brackets which were themselves fashioned in the form of either panelled or fluted columns. At the foot of the figurehead was the 'trayle board' (trailboard) which was decorated with seahorses and dolphins carved in bas relief.

The sides of the ship were relatively plain with a simple painted frieze running the full length of the ship above the sheer rail. Similarly a frieze was painted above the drift rails fore and aft. On this frieze there were voluted foliage designs picked out with what looked like gold paint, but which was in reality more likely to have been yellow ochre. The background of the frieze was either black or aqua blue and may, in some cases, have possibly been red. The colour schemes on contemporary models are not always a reliable way of determining the actual pigments used at the period and therefore the colour scheme I have suggested is purely speculative. For practical reasons black would have been the most likely colour for the background of the frieze.

The decoration at the stern was far more elaborate. The tafferal or uppermost portion generally carried a coat-of-arms centrally supported by reclining cherubs. Sometimes there were two coats-of-arms, in which case the figures were usually reclining Gods or Greek heroes. Flagstaffs and weaponry decorated the base of the tafferal. At each side adjacent to the stern lights were quarter figures of warriors bearing arms, which surmounted mythological fish or dolphins which formed part of the lower finishing.

Between the stern lights (windows) were a series of either panelled or fluted pillars supporting a lintel of heavy moulding. A similar moulding was employed for the sill of the lights, which also served as the top edge of the upper counter. The upper counter was painted with a background the same colour as the friezework displayed along the ship's side. This counter was divided into two friezes, the uppermost like that above the drift rails. The lower frieze consisted of voluted acanthus leaves with a central band of laurels supported by nude maidens.

The pillars and moulding of the quarter lights were consistent with those at the stern lights. The upper and lower finishing were decorated with carvings of acanthus leaves. Three plumes of acanthus supported the sill of the quarter light, their lower ends terminating in a scroll. The upper finishing was fashioned in the same manner but the other way up.

Some contemporary models carry three stern lanterns and others only one. This makes it difficult to determine what was normal practice. From inspection of various models it can be asserted that in all probability those vessels built earlier bore three lanterns, those later, one. However, some vessels carried two lanterns.

LAYOUT

The *Blandford* was officially referred to as a 'single-decker', for her armament was carried on one deck only. This was called the upper (or main) deck. Her armament consisted of twenty 6-pounder carriage guns, but there is reason to believe that at one point in her career she may have carried a number of swivel guns in addition to her main armament. Unlike most other vessels of the period all her cannon were exposed to the weather.

Along the centre line of the upper deck were quite a number of gratings which gave access to the deck below or served to ventilate the ship. The section of this deck between the main and the fore mast was commonly known as the 'waist' and was used for stowing the ship's boats, spare spars and the sweeps (if carried). Aft of the main mast was the upper portion of the main capstan which was employed for raising the anchor, warping the ship and lifting weights as required. The steering wheel was placed abaft the mizzen mast under the overhang of the quarterdeck. At the extreme fore end of the upper deck was a short closed-in area under the forecastle. Here the ship's heads (latrines) were situated, built into the two roundhouses, which were integral with the ship's side. The area aft under the quarterdeck contained the captain's quarters, the compartments being divided off by a transverse bulkhead. There were a number of fittings fastened along the bulwarks of this deck, which were used for the securing of various important ropes such as sheets and braces. Other fittings included the galley flue and the main and fore topsail and jeer bitts.

Below the main deck was the lower deck which was often referred to as the berthing deck as it was used for the accommodation of the ship's company and the remaining officers. At the extreme fore end were the hawse holes through which the anchor cables passed. To prevent any inadvertant ingress of sea water from the hawse holes spreading throughout the entire deck, a small 'dwarf' bulkhead was erected across the deck. It closed off a small area known as the 'manger' as livestock were often kept in it. Incorporated with the after side of the manger was the step for the bowsprit which consisted of two baulks of timber with a mortice cut between them to receive the tenon of the mast.

Aft of the step were two sets of riding bitts, to which the anchor cables were secured when the ship was riding at anchor. The foremost pair were a little unorthodox in design as they were not fitted with a cross piece. The cross piece type was fitted on vessels where space was not at a premium but on the *Blandford* the foremost pair could only be fitted either side of the fore mast. In the vicinity of the main mast were the ship's pumps. There were two elm tree pumps for domestic use and fire-fighting and two chain pumps for pumping out the bilges. Abaft was the main capstan which was integral with that on the deck above, the part on the lower deck being employed for weighing anchor.

The remaining part of the lower deck consisted of the gunroom which served as both cabin space and a wardroom for the officers. The gunroom was divided off from the rest of the deck by a transverse bulkhead.

Below this deck were fore and aft hold and platform decks. At the extreme

fore end was the fore peak which served as a sail room and boatswain's store. On the fore platform at the centre line was the galley space with its brick firehearth and galley stove. Either side were store rooms for the carpenter and the boatswain. The fore part of the hold was used as the cable tier for the anchor hawsers, the remaining part of the hold was used for general provisions and cordage.

The after platform was divided off into a series of store rooms – the slop room, fish room, spirit room and captain's store room. The after section of the platform was occupied by the magazine. This compartment was divided into a powder room and filling room, the latter being a store for ready-use cartridges. The entire magazine was illuminated from a separate lightroom where an external lantern was placed at a window. Both the bulkheads and the deck of the magazine were built with a double layer of planking to prevent the ingress of damp and water. The remaining after section of the hold consisted of the bread room, access being attained from the after platform by a passageway on the port side of the magazine.

ACCOMMODATION

The accommodation aboard a 20-gun ship was relatively cramped as was the case on all small ships. However, the 20-gun ship had one advantage: all the armament was situated on the open upper deck, therefore the living space on the lower deck was far better than that of the crew of a ship of the line.

At the after end of the upper deck, beneath the quarterdeck was the captain's cabin. This was relatively spacious compared to the rest of the ship. It was divided into two compartments, a day cabin where he would eat and conduct his everyday business and a small sleeping cabin. Access was through a door on the port side of the main bulkhead. This appears to have been common on all 20-gun ships. The day cabin was illuminated by daylight from both the stern lights and the two quarter badges. Further ventilation and light could also be admitted through the two aftermost gun ports, and the starboard one for his sleeping berth. No guns were fitted at these two ports but provision was made should it be necessary to do so. All of the bulkheads in this vicinity could be easily removed which not only provided more space to operate the ship during action, but reduced the danger of splinters which accounted for most injuries when the ship came under fire.

Below, on the lower deck or berthing deck as it was often referred to, the accommodation was divided in two. Aft in the gunroom were the officers, while forward the remainder of the crew ate and slept. The gunroom served as the wardroom around which usually four, or sometimes six cabins were fitted. These were used by the ship's lieutenant, the lieutenant of marines, the master and the surgeon. It is not known whether additional cabins for the purser etc were fitted in this area or just forward of the wardroom. On some vessels these cabins were made from light deal panels, on others, canvas stretched over a frame. On the *Blandford* however, there appears to be no reason why these cabins would need to be dismantled, as this deck would not have been cleared for action, thus cabins built with wooden panels would probably have been more common. Both the captain and the officers slept in cots suspended from the deck head, there personal belongings being kept in a chest which served both as a table and a seat. In the middle of the wardroom was a large table which probably served as a chart table for the Master when not being used for meals.

The remainder of the crew lived and ate forward of the wardroom bulkhead. They slept in hammocks suspended from hooks driven into the beams. As a rule each man was allotted 14 inches of space, but in fact there was a little more comfort, for half the crew would be on watch at once. The warrant officers such as the gunner, boatswain and quartermaster, etc divided themselves off from the rest by hanging canvas screens to form their own mess. Other members of the crew who did not actually work the ship, such as the captain's clerk and servants and the carpenter probably found their own 'niches' in their store rooms which were situated on either the fore or the after platforms in the hold.

The crew ate at long tables which hung from the beams, and sat on wooden forms. Food was cooked on a brick firehearth built in the centre of the fore platform. The stove consisted of two copper kettles where the cook boiled up salt pork or beef. The smoke from the fire passed up through a flue to the upper deck. In later years the galley was placed under the forecastle and instead of having a brick firehearth it was made of iron. The latrines or 'heads' were situated in the two roundhouses built into the ship's side under the forecastle. One would have been used by the officers and would have been furnished with a screen. A piss-dale was also fitted on each bulwark just aft of the second gunport. In later years when these vessels were modified and quarter galleries replaced the badges, the officer's heads were moved to one of the galleries, so no doubt the warrant officers and petty officers commandeered one of the roundhouses forward.

It was usual practice to place the hammocks in nettings around the upper deck bulwarks, when they were not in use below, to give protection in action. However, there appears to be no evidence to suggest that hammock cranes and netting were on *Blandford*. Therefore it can be assumed that the hammocks were generally stowed below. These vessels never or rarely got into heavy action where this form of protection was necessary.

STEERING

The steering system was a relatively simple affair comprising a rudder, tiller, tiller quadrant and steering wheel. It was operated by the tiller rope and the tiller which acted as a lever.

The rudder or 'rother' as it was often called acted as a surface plane over which the water passed. Any alteration made in the angle of the rudder affected the water flow, thereby turning the ship. The rudder was hinged by gudgeons and pintles to the after side of the stern post, around which it rotated on its axis. The head of the rudder stock was fashioned with a mortice to receive the after end of the tiller. Iron hoops and strappings were fitted to strengthen this part of the stock.

The tiller was made from ash, chosen for its properties of withstanding strain and shock when the rudder was hit by heavy seas. The fore end of the tiller was supported by the tiller quadrant which was a curved beam fitted under the upper deck beams. The arc of the quadrant corresponded with that produced by the sweep of the tiller, thus the tiller was supported throughout its entire traverse travel.

The steering wheel was a relatively recent innovation and had only been in general use for less than two decades. On 20-gun ships it was situated abaft the mizzen mast on the upper deck. When these ships were modified by the quarterdeck being extended forward, the helm position was raised to the quarterdeck. The helm consisted of a single spoked wheel connected to a horizontal barrel, the whole assembly being supported by two short stanchions, one forward, one aft.

The tiller rope was turned around the barrel about seven times. Each end then passed down to the deck below via sheaves set vertically in the deck. The ropes then passed to their respective tiller blocks fitted at the ship's side and

thence to the fore end of the tiller where they were secured. Alternatively, they passed through eyebolts on the tiller and to the tensioning tackle blocks. Though tensioning tackle may have been used it was not common during this period. Secondary steering was obtained by use of the rudder pendants attached to a ringbolt fitted on the hance of the rudder.

GROUND TACKLE
Ground tackle is the collective name given to the anchors and their associated equipment; capstans are also covered in this section. The 20-gun ships of this era generally carried two bower anchors, two sheet anchors and a kedge anchor. A stream anchor was sometimes carried if required. It was used in combination with the kedge for warping the ship in narrow channels or when becalmed. They could be suspended under the ship's boats and easily transported.

The bower anchors were at all times secured to their respective cables for instant use and were stowed hanging from the catheads and lashed to the fore channel. The sheet anchors were also secured to the fore channel, the kedge being lashed to the port sheet anchor. During this period all anchors were furnished with wooden stocks, made in two halves joined together by bolts and iron hoops. The function of the stock was to 'trip' the anchor thereby allowing one of the palms to embed itself into the seabed.

Most ships had between five and six anchor cables but it can be assumed that only three or four cables were actually carried aboard 20-gun ships due to the relatively limited storage space. Each cable for this class of ship was $13\frac{1}{2}$ inches in circumference and 120 fathoms in length. A lighter cable which was far easier to transport was carried for the kedge anchor when it was used to warp the ship.

The anchor cables entered the ship via the hawse holes at the fore end of the lower deck and were transferred to the cable tier in the hold by means of a second cable of lesser diameter. The ship's boys joined the two cables with temporary lashings called 'nippings'. A second cable had to be used because in most cases the anchor cable was of too great a diameter to pass round the capstan. During the first half of the eighteenth century there were two methods of moving the anchor cable both involving another cable, one of which was called the vyol, the other a messenger. In both cases the ends of the cables were spliced together to form a continuous loop of rope. It appears that it was more practical to use a vyol when the capstan was sited before the main mast. The vyol was passed through a snatch block rigged to the main mast and then to the capstan forward. The messenger passed directly aft to the capstan situated abaft the main mast and then returned forward to the hawse holes. The capstan on 20-gun ships was usually placed aft of the main mast, therefore it can be assumed that in the case of the *Blandford*, a messenger was used. However, it could be argued that because the anchor cable itself had a relatively small diameter it was lead directly to the capstan. Not only would this have been less time consuming but it would have reduced the number of cables carried.

Blandford's capstan was double-tiered with a common spindle. The uppermost capstan was fitted with whelps and a drum head. The whelps were fitted to increase the diameter of the drum and to allow the rope to tighten, giving greater friction and reducing any slip. The drum head was slotted to receive the ten capstan bars. The lower capstan at this period did not have a drum head and consisted only of a number of whelps and the pawls. The pawls acted as a form of ratchet which worked against the feet of the whelps to prevent the capstan reversing direction. The position of each pawl could be altered,

TABLE 4: SHEET ANCHOR DIMENSIONS FOR A SHIP OF 364 TONS BURDEN

	Ft	In
Shank length	12	2
Maximum shank thickness		$7\frac{1}{2}$
Minimum shank thickness		$5\frac{1}{2}$
Length of the square	1	11
Position of the nut	1	3
Square of the nut		$1^{51}/_{100}$
Inner diameter of the ring	1	3
Thickness of the ring		3
Hole diameter for the ring in the shank		$3^1/_{10}$
Length of the crown		$8^7/_{20}$
Length of the arm	4	$0^6/_{10}$
Length of the fluke	2	$5\frac{1}{2}$
Breadth of the fluke	1	9
Thickness of the fluke		$1^9/_{10}$
Length of the bill		$6^9/_{10}$
Square of the arm at the fluke		$4^6/_{10}$
Rounding of the fluke		$7^6/_{100}$
Clutching of the arm	2	$4^1/_{10}$

Arms	$\frac{3}{4}$ × the length of the shank and formed to an arc of a circle which is $^2/_5$ of the arm broad
Circumference of the throat	$^1/_5$ × length of the shank
Length of the stock	length of the shank plus half the diameter of the ring
Length of the parallel section of the stock	$^1/_6$ of its overall length
Stops	set at a position $^1/_{24}$ of the length of the shank from one end

allowing the capstan to haul or veer as necessary.

Each capstan bar was 7 feet long and 3 inches square in section. In most cases they were made from ash. There were ten bars in total so with three men at each bar a total of thirty seamen could weigh the anchor. Additional men could assist by pulling on the swifter, a rope passing around the ends of the bars. The capstan was also used for hoisting in stores, raising yards and so on, and hoisting the ship's boats.

Once the anchor had broken surface the catblock was hooked to the anchor ring and the anchor was hoisted to the cathead, or 'catted' as it was known. Once this was done the anchor was 'fished' by means of the fish davit and secured to the fore channel.

PUMPS
Two types of pumps were fitted aboard the 20-gun ship, the chain pump and the elm tree pump, each serving a separate function. The chain pump was used primarily for removing water from the bilges which accumulated at the lowest point of the limber passages at the well of the ship. Although referred to as one pump, it in fact consisted of two individual pumps which shared a cistern sited on the lower deck a little abaft the main mast. Each pump consisted of two tubes, a back case and a return case; the latter was often referred to as the working chamber. Fitted at the top and bottom of these casings was a sprocket wheel around which passed a continuous loop of chain to which circular pieces of leather backed with an iron plate or 'saucer' were attached. The uppermost sprocket wheel was turned (towards the centre line of the ship) by a series of crank handles which engaged with the spindle of the sprocket wheel. Additional crank handles could be fitted to increase the number of operators. As each leather washer entered the limber passage it scooped up water and lifted it to the cistern via the working chamber. The water level in the cistern would rise and eventually water would flow out through the pump dale to the scupper and was thus discharged overboard.

During this period both the chain and the sprocket wheel were simple in design and it was not uncommon for the chain to break or the crutches forming the sprockets to foul up with the chain. The wooden block forming the sprocket wheel hubs was generally made from elm. The lower wheel was not always made in the form of a sprocket but sometimes left simply as a roller. The pump was relatively efficient but it was to be another forty years before William Cole modified the moving components and increased the pump's output.

The elm tree pump was employed for domestic uses, washing down the decks and fire-fighting. It took water directly from the sea and was operated with a handle or 'brake' which produced the reciprocating action necessary for its operation. The casing of the pump was made from a single bored out elm tree. The lower end passed through the bottom of the ship, the upper end terminated at the upper deck, where the water was discharged. Alternatively water could be discharged on the lower deck by simply removing the cover from an outlet port.

Two valve 'boxes' were fitted within the pump's bore, the lower valve box being fixed, at a position approximately one-third of the way from the bottom. The other valve box was connected to the brake by an iron rod, often called the 'spear'. Both valve boxes were fitted with a 'clapper' non-return valve. The lower 'box' could be removed for repair by hooking up a staple fitted to its top. Iron hoops were fitted around the casing to prevent splitting.

ARMAMENT

The *Blandford* was armed with twenty 6-pounder carriage guns, the size and weight of which were authorised by the Gun Establishment of 1716. This stated that all 20-gun sixth Rates were to carry 6-pounders with a length of 7 feet 6 inches and weighing eighteen hundredweight. The cannon was made from cast iron and bored out smooth to a diameter of $3\frac{1}{2}$ inches. The diameter of the shot was generally one-fifth less than the bore of the gun and therefore in this case was approximately $2\frac{7}{8}$ inches diameter. The charge required to fire a 6-pounder was between one third and one half of the weight of the shot. Therefore a single broadside would have expended between 40 and 60 pounds of gunpowder. Firing a cannon was somewhat precarious and was done by using a slow match held on a linstock which was placed at the touch hole.

The gun was mounted on a wooden carriage made from elm. This type of timber was used for two reasons: firstly it did not splinter into small shards, thereby reducing the degree of injury caused by splinter wounds; secondly, it had the property of withstanding shock – ideal in view of the force of the gun's recoil. The carriage consisted of two side cheeks, a front transom and a bed which carried the quoin. The quoin was a wedge-shaped block of timber placed under the breech and was used to either elevate or depress the gun as required. The overall length of the carriage was generally three-fifths of the length of the gun itself, and in thickness it was equal to the bore diameter of the gun. At the fore and after end of the carriage were two axletrees on which wooden wheels called trucks, made from oak, were fitted. These could be removed if necessary; the removal of the back trucks gave greater elevation to the gun. The gun barrel was held to the carriage by iron hinges known as cap squares which fitted over the trunnions and were locked down by a pin inserted in the keep plate.

Each gun was furnished with gun tackle, traversing tackle and a breeching rope. The breeching was a good-quality stout hemp rope which secured the gun to the bulwark and took the strain of the recoil. Its inboard end was passed around the cascable behind the breech of the gun. Fitted either side of the

TABLE 5: **GUN TACKLE SIZES FOR A 6-POUNDER**

	Rope circumference (Ins)	Length of rope (Ft)
Breeching	$4\frac{1}{2}$	24
Gun tackle	2	30
Traversing tackle	2	26–30

carriage was the gun tackle which was used to run the gun out ready to fire. At the rear of the carriage was the traversing tackle. This served two functions; one was simply to haul the gun back for reloading, the other, by transferring the tackle to an adjacent ringbolt in the deck, to make oblique fire possible.

Swivel guns were fitted on some of the Sixth Rates during this period. One model in the National Maritime Museum at Greenwich, of either the *Blandford* or the *Lyme*, is fitted out with twenty-two swivels. The standard half-pounder swivel gun at this period was 2 feet $6\frac{1}{4}$ inches long, weighed 46 pounds, and had a bore of 15 inches diameter. Each gun was mounted on an iron yoke which was set into a timber pedestal. The pedestals were usually bolted to the outboard side of the bulwark, but in some cases the gun was supported by an iron stanchion set into the deck. The main function of the weapon was anti-personnel, and cannister shot was often used as an alternative to solid shot.

Three 20-gun ships, the *Seaford* and *Shoreham* of the *Blandford* type, and the earlier *Solebay*, were converted to bomb vessels. Although this form of mortar had been in naval service since the latter part of the seventeenth century an improved design was introduced after successful testing had been carried out at Woolwich in June 1726. The advantage of the mortar was that it fired an explosive shell in a high trajectory, which was very useful for bombardment of ships in harbour, shore-side installations and fortresses. Due to the sparsity of sources on this subject, it is not known how many were carried on the converted 20s.

The mortar consisted of a short heavy barrel mounted on a large solid bed. The barrel at this time was made of either brass or cast iron and was approximately 5 feet in length and had a bore of 13 inches. The bed was made from heavy baulks of elm. The type employed at this time was designed by William Ogbourne, the master carpenter at Woolwich. It was made to rotate and therefore could be classified as the forerunner of the modern turret gun. Considerable structural alterations were necessary in order to convert vessels not built to withstand the weight and recoil action of the mortar. This involved strengthening the hull by fitting riders in the hold and deck beams of greater scantling. All of this work would have been expensive, as the following list illustrates. *Solebay* converted 16–28 June 1726 at a cost of £1070 12s 0d; *Shoreham* converted March–15 April 1727 cost not known but probably similar, and *Seaford* converted 2–15 March 1726/27 at a cost of £1010 3s 7d.

SHOT

The British Navy's preference was for solid round shot, but alternative types for destroying masting and rigging were occasionally used. These took the form of bar shot, chain shot and expanding shot. For anti-personnel use, either cannister or grape shot was employed. Both types had a 'spray' effect, cutting down the enemy. The shot used in the mortar was generally in the form of a hollow iron ball filled with explosive. A fuse was inserted and lit prior to loading it. The timing of the firing could be determined by the length of fuse

woven in the timing cone inserted in the shell or 'bomb'. By trial and error and adjustments in trajectory an explosion on impact could be achieved.

MASTS AND SPARS

All 20-gun Sixth Rates were ship-rigged, which meant that they had three masts and a bowsprit. The fore and main masts were complete (in other words they had a lower mast, topmast and topgallant mast), whereas the mizzen mast had no topgallant. The bowsprit was extended by a jibboom in order to carry the jib sail.

During the early eighteenth century most masts were made from a single tree, with additions such as the cheeks and the bibs fitted separately. Generally Riga or New England pine was preferred for mast manufacture due to its girth and length. The heel of each mast was stepped into a large baulk of timber fashioned with a suitable mortice which was bolted firmly astride the keelson. The bowsprit, due to its angle or 'steeve' was stepped into a vertical block situated on the lower deck a little afore the fore mast.

At the head of each lower mast was a flat platform called a top, which was supported by two crosstrees set transversely and two trestletrees set fore and aft. The heel of the topmast was set between the trestletrees and located by an iron pin called a fid. The topmast was further supported by a block, known as a mast cap, fitted to the lower mast head. The topgallant masts were supported in the same manner. The jibboom was retained by a cap at the extremity of the bowsprit and its heel was set into a block forming a saddle over the top surface of the bowsprit. The yards, with the exception of the topgallants and spritsail, were round except for their centre section which was octagonal. Two sling cleats were fitted at the centre to retain the slings and yard parrel ropes. Cleats were also fitted at the yardarms for securing various blocks and the sail. The lower (or course) yards of the main and fore masts were made from two pieces, scarphed together with battens nailed on the flats of the octagonal section to give additional strength.

The tops fitted to the lower masts served a twofold function: they spread the shrouds of the respective topmast and provided a suitable platform from which sharpshooters could fire their muskets during action. From this position they could easily pick out a target. The top was constructed from light boards set up on the crosstrees. A rail was fitted at the after side to provide some degree of safety. The crosstrees fitted at the topmast head remained unplanked but were still used as a lookout post despite being exposed and precarious.

STANDING RIGGING

The standing rigging included all of the cordage that braced and supported the masts from aft, forward, and laterally. These ropes were called backstays, forestays and shrouds respectively. Much preparation and care was taken in setting up this rigging. All of the cordage was well tarred to protect it from the elements and some ropes were further protected from wear by serving, worming or parcelling as necessary.

The fore and main mast lower stays were set up with a suitably formed eye which was passed over the mast head. The stay then passed forward and downward at an oblique angle to either a collar or deck fastening. A heart was seized into the lower end of the stay. A similar heart was seized to the collar and the two hearts were then lashed together by a lanyard. The lower end of the mizzen stay was secured to the lower part of the main mast by deadeyes and lanyards.

The topmast and topgallant mast stays were secured in the same manner as those of the mizzen stay, except that a block was used, the fall of the stay passing down to the deck. Each block was fastened to its respective mast head by a pendant.

TABLE 6: **MAST AND YARD DIMENSIONS FOR THE 20-GUN SHIPS OF 1719**

Mast	Length		Diameter	
	Ft	In	Ft	In
Main mast	68	6	1	8½
Fore mast	61	8	1	6½
Mizzen mast	54	10		11¼
Bowsprit	40	8	1	4½
Main topmast	39	9		11⅞
Fore topmast	37	3		11⅞
Mizzen topmast	27	10		7¾
Main topgallant	19	6		6⅛
Fore topgallant	18	4		6⅛
Jibboom	22	4		6½
Ensign staff	23	6		4¾
Jack staff	11	9		3

Yards	Length		Diameter	
	Ft	In	Ft	In
Main yard	60	6	1	2
Fore yard	52	11	1	0½
Mizzen yard	50	5		9
Crossjack	38	6		7⅞
Main topsail yard	44	0		9⅛
Fore topsail yard	38	6		8
Mizzen topsail yard	28	10		5¾
Main topgallant yard	25	8		5⅛
Fore topgallant yard	22	6		4½
Spritsail yard	38	6		8

DIMENSIONS OF THE CROSSTREES

Mast	Length		Breadth	Depth
	Ft	In	In	In
Main mast	12	6	6¾	4½
Fore mast	11	7	6⅛	4¼
Mizzen mast	6	10	4	2½
Main topmast	5	2½	2¾	2¼
Fore topmast	4	11	2½	2⅛

DIMENSION OF THE TRESTLETREES

Mast	Length		Breadth	Depth
	Ft	In	In	In
Main mast	9	7	6¾	9⅛
Fore mast	8	11	6⅛	8½
Mizzen mast	5	10	4	4⅞
Main topmast	3	11	2¾	3¾
Fore topmast	3	8	2¼	3½

DIMENSIONS OF THE MAST CAPS

Mast	Length		Breadth		Depth
	Ft	In	Ft	In	In
Main mast	3	11½	1	11¾	10½
Fore mast	3	11½	1	11¾	9½
Mizzen mast	2	7	1	3½	6⅝
Main topmast	2	2	1	1	5⅛
Fore topmast	2	0½	1	0¾	4⅞
Bowsprit	2	11	1	2	6¼

TABLE 7: **RIGGING SIZES**

Note. All dimensions are of the rope's circumference.

FORE STAYS

Item	Stay (Ins)	Stay collar (Ins)	Lanyard (Ins)	Worming (Ins)
Fore stay	9½	8½	3	1
Fore preventer stay	6½	5½	2	½
Fore topmast stay	4¾	3¾	1½	–
Fore topmast preventer stay	3½	2¾	1	–
Fore topgallant stay	2¼	–	¾	–
Main stay	10½	7½	3¼	1
Main preventer stay	7¼	5¼	2¼	½
Main topmast stay	5¼	4	1¾	–
Main topmast preventer stay	4	3	1¼	–
Main topgallant stay	2½	–	1	–
Mizzen stay	5½	4½	2	½
Mizzen preventer stay	5½	4¼	2	½
Mizzen topmast stay	2¾	2	1	–
Bobstay	4¾	4½	2¼	–

SHROUDS

Item	Size (Ins)	Deadeye Lanyard Size (Ins)	No of Pairs (Ins)
Fore lower shrouds	5¾	3	5
Fore topmast shrouds	3¾	2	3
Fore futtock shrouds	3¾	–	3
Fore topgallantmast shrouds	2¼	1¼	2
Main lower shrouds	6¼	3¼	6
Main topmast shrouds	4	2	3
Main futtock shrouds	4	2	3
Main topgallantmast shrouds	2½	1¼	2
Mizzen lower shrouds	4½	2¼	3
Mizzen topmast shrouds	2¾	1¼	2
Mizzen futtock shrouds	2¾	1¼	2
Bowsprit shrouds	4	2	1
Bowsprit gammon lashing	4	–	1

BACKSTAYS

Item	Size (Ins)	Lanyard size (Ins)
Fore backstay	5¾	3
Main backstay	6½	3¼
Mizzen backstay	4½	2¼
Fore topmast backstay	3¾	2
Main topmast backstay	4	2
Mizzen topmast backstay	2¾	1¼
Fore topgallant backstay	2¼	1
Main topgallant backstay	2½	1¼

THE RIGGING TO THE LOWER YARDS

Rigging	Fore Yard (Ins)	Main Yard (Ins)
Tie	4¾	5¼
Jeer	4¾	7
Jeer falls	2¼	2½
Slings	2½	4
Parrel rope	3	4
Brace pendants	3¼	3½
Brace	2¼	2½
Lifts	3	2½
Lift span	3	3½
Yard tackle pendant	3¾	4
Yard tackle	2¼	2½
Yard tackle tricing line	1	1¼
Footrope	2¼	2½
Footrope lanyards	1	1
Leechline legs and falls	2	2
Leechline strop	2	2

LOWER YARDS (cont)

	Fore Yard (Ins)	Main Yard (Ins)
Buntline legs and falls	1¾	2
Bowlines and bridles	2¼	2½
Reef pendants	2¼	2½
Reef tackles	1	1¼
Reefing lines	1	1
Clew garnets	2	2
Sheets	3¾	4
Tack, at widest point	4¼	5¼
Outer stunsail halyard	2¼	2½
Inner stunsail halyards	2	2
Stunsail boom topping lift and guys	2	2

THE RIGGING TO THE CROSSJACK YARD

Item	Ins
Slings	3½
Truss pendant	3¼
Truss pendant falls	2¾
Lifts	3½
Lift span	1
Footrope	2¼
Footrope lanyard	1¼
Brace pendants	2¾
Brace	2½
Jeer	2

RIGGING TO THE TOPSAIL YARDS

Item	Fore (Ins)	Main (Ins)	Mizzen (Ins)
Ties	3	4¼	2¾
Runner of the tie	2½	3½	2¼
Halyard	2	2¾	2
Parrel rope	2	2¼	1¾
Lifts	2¼	2¾	2
Footropes	2½	2¾	1¾
Footrope lanyards	1	1¼	¾
Brace pendants	3	3	2
Brace	2	2	1¾
Leechlines	1½	1¾	1
Buntlines	1¾	2¼	1
Bowlines and bridles	2	2¼	1
Reef tackle pendants	2¼	2¾	1½
Reef tackle falls	1½	1½	1
Clewlines	2	2¼	2
Sheets	4¼	4¾	2¾
Stunsail halyards, sheets and tacks	2¼	2¼	–
Stunsail downhauler and boom tackle	1½	1½	–

THE RIGGING TO THE TOPGALLANT YARDS

Item	Fore (Ins)	Main (Ins)
Ties	2¼	2¼
Halyard	1	1¼
Parrel rope	1¼	1¼
Lifts	1½	1½
Footrope	1½	1¾
Footrope lanyard	¾	¾
Brace pendants	1½	1½
Brace	1¼	1¼
Buntlines	¾	1
Bowlines and bridles	1	1¼
Clewlines	1	1¼
Sheets	2¼	2½

TABLE 7: **RIGGING SIZES**

RIGGING TO THE SPRITSAIL YARD

Item	Ins
Parrel rope	3
Slings	3¾
Halyard	3¾
Lanyard	1
Garnet	2
Standing lifts	2
Standing lift lanyards	1
Brace pendant	3
Brace	2¼
Running lift	2
Sheet pendants	3
Sheet strop	2¼
Clewlines	2
Footrope	2¼
Reef points	1
Buntlines	2

THE RIGGING TO THE MIZZEN YARD

Item	Ins
Parrel rope	3
Slings	5
Ties	3¾
Tie falls	3
Jeers	5
Lifts	2
Lift span and falls	2
Bowlines	3
Sheets	4
Foot brails	2¼
Peak and throat brails	1¼
Lacing to the yard	1
Tack	3

RIGGING OF THE JIB SAIL

Item	Ins
Jib sail stay	2¼
Stay fall	1½
Stay tackle	1½
Halyard	2¼
Sheet pendants	2¼
Sheets	2
Tacks and whips	1½
Downhauler	2

RIGGING TO THE FORE TOPMAST SAIL

Item	Ins
Staysail stay	2½
Lanyard	2
Tackle	1½
Halyard	1¾
Sheet pendants	2¼
Sheet pendant whips	1½
Tacks and sheets	2
Downhauler	2

RIGGING OF THE MAIN TOPMAST STAYSAIL

Item	Ins
Staysail stay	2½
Staysail sheet pendants	2½
Staysail sheets	2¼
Staysail sheet whips	2
Staysail halyards	2½
Staysail tacks	2¼
Downhauler	1¼

RIGGING TO THE MAIN TOPGALLANT STAYSAIL

Item	Ins
Staysail stay	2
Halyard	1½
Sheet pendants	1½
Sheets	1¼
Sheet pendant whips	1¼
Tacks and downhaulers	1

RIGGING OF THE MIZZEN STAYSAIL

Item	Ins
Halyard	2¼
Sheet pendants	2¼
Sheets and tack	2¼
Downhauler	1¼

RIGGING OF THE MIZZEN TOPMAST STAYSAIL

Item	Ins
Staysail halyard	1¼
Staysail sheets	1¼
Tacks	1
Downhauler	1

SIZES OF MISCELLANEOUS ROPES AND CABLES

Item	Ins
Cat fall	3¼
Back rope	2
Cathead stopper	3¼
Shank painter tail	4¼
Fish pendant	5¼
Fish pendant tackle	2½
Anchor cable – sheet and bower	13½
Spare cables	12
Kedge anchor cable	8
Messenger or vyol	8
Nippers, hook ropes and ring stoppers	1¼
Swifters	1¼
Bittstoppers	5¼
Anchor buoy rope	4¾
Anchor buoy slings	2
Rudder pendants	4¼
Rudder pendant falls	2
Tiller rope	2½
Gunport tackles	2

The bowsprit was rigged with a bobstay which passed from the forestay collar to the knee of the head. The lower end was in the shape of an eye and the upper end was secured to deadeyes. The backstays were rigged from the mast heads down to the channel or backstay stool on the ship's side. The upper end was in the shape of an eye which fitted over the mast head, the lower end was seized to a deadeye. A similar deadeye was fastened to the channel board or stool, the two being lashed together by a lanyard.

The lower shrouds passed from their respective channels to the mast head. They were joined into a pair by an eye which fitted over the mast head and was spliced in the bights. The tail end of the shroud was seized to a deadeye which was fastened to its counterpart on the channel by a lanyard. The lower deadeye was secured to the ship's side by a chain plate. The topmast and topgallant mast shrouds were set up in the same manner with their respective deadeyes fitted at the sides of the tops or the crosstrees. Futtock shrouds were rigged from the lower shrouds to the deadeye plates of the topmast shrouds. In the same manner futtock shrouds were also rigged from the topmast shrouds to the crosstrees. Once all of the shrouds were set up they were 'rattled down' with ratlines which formed footholds for the seamen to scale the masts.

The bowsprit was also fitted with two shrouds, one either side, passing from the forestay collar to the ship's side. The upper end was secured to the collar by deadeyes and a lanyard. A hook was seized to the lower end of each shroud, the hook being fastened and moused to an eyebolt fitted a little above the main wale, aft of the hawse holes.

RUNNING RIGGING

This comprised all the ropework which was employed for manipulating the yards and sails. In general this cordage was untarred to prevent it jamming in the blocks.

The rigging to the lower yards consisted of parrels, slings, jeers and lifts. Their function was to raise, lower and support the yard. Braces were rigged to the yardarms to rotate the yard around its axis on the mast. The topsail, topgallant and spritsail yards were rigged in the same manner as the lower yards, the only difference being that ties were used instead of the jeer tackle.

The amount of rigging to the sails themselves was considerable, thus for simplicity I have divided it into two categories: that which furled the sails up and that which held the sails taut and in position when in use. Additionally, most sails were rigged with reef tackle which was used to raise the sail a short distance when taking in reefs to shorten sail. For furling the sails, clewlines, buntlines and leechlines were used, each line pulling the sail upward and inward. The mizzen sail was rigged with peak, throat and foot brails for furling it instead of buntlines. Tacks, sheets, bowlines and bridles were employed to hold the sail in position when in use. Most of the sails had reef points that were used to shorten them as required.

The fore and aft staysails and jib sail were, with the exception of those on the mizzen mast, set up on staysail stays, the upper ends of which were seized to their respective stays. Each sail was raised on its stay by a halyard and lowered by a downhauler. Tacks and sheets were rigged to each sail so that it could be positioned as required for tacking or wearing ship.

Each of the studdingsail booms and yards were rigged with halyards, topping lifts and guy ropes. The sails each had their respective halyards, sheets and tacks, the topmast stunsail having a downhauler.

THE SAILS

Two types of sails were employed on 20-gun ships: square sails which were set transversely, bent to the yards, and a number of triangular sails, generally called staysails, set up fore and aft on the stays. Both types of sail were made up of strips (or cloths) of canvas sewn together, each strip being a standard two feet wide. Each edge of the sail was stiffened with a rope stitched to the seams; this was called the bolt rope.

The sides of a square sail were called the head, foot, and leech, the latter being the two perpendicular sides. The same terminology was applied to the bolt ropes, ie the head bolt rope, and so on, and to the three-sided sails though there was only one leech.

Additional cloths, or linings as they were called, were sewn at varying positions on each sail to give extra strength, or where excessive wear would occur. The linings were generally placed where there were buntlines, or reef points, along the leeches and where the foot of the sail came into contact with the fore rim of the tops. Along the leeches and the foot of the sail small rope eyes called cringles were worked into the bolt ropes. To these various parts of the rigging were secured, such as the buntlines, leech lines, reef tackle and the bridles and bowlines. Eyes were fitted at each corner of the sail. Those at the top two corners were called earings. From these a lashing was passed to the yardarm cleat. The tack and sheet blocks were fastened at the lower two corners, or clews as they were called.

The seam across the head of the sail had small holes, usually two per sail cloth, through which robbands passed. These were short lengths of rope which passed between the holes and around the yard securing the whole breadth of the sail. The ends of the rope were fastened with a reef knot. Reef points were placed as appropriate along the fore and after sides of the sail, and like the holes for the robbands there were two to every cloth. Short ropes were passed through these points so when shortening sail the two ends of the reefs were tied together over the top of the yard.

The fashion in which the fore and aft staysails were rigged varied according to their position. Some were bent onto the actual stay and others were set up on their own staysail stay. These sails had the necessary earings and clews but with the exception of the mizzen sail did not have cringles.

In addition to the standard set of sails, studdingsails (sometimes abbreviated to stunsails) were carried for use in light winds. It appears that a lower and a topmast stunsail were carried only on the fore and main masts. Sources contain little precise information on these sails.

Although there are no original sail plans of any consequence for the 20-gun ship of the early eighteenth century, I estimate the total sail area including the stunsails was 15,084 square feet. The individual estimated sail areas are shown in Table 8.

BOATS

In all probability, the *Blandford* only carried one 27-foot pinnace as authorised in the 1719 Establishment. However, according to the recommendations forwarded by the Navy Board in March 1714/15, vessels of 20 or 24 guns were to carry a 27-foot pinnace and a 17-foot yawl. The pinnace had been in service use for quite some time and had proved very suitable for various duties such as watering ship, conveying stores, personnel or raiding parties.

TABLE 8: **ESTIMATED SAIL AREAS OF A 20-GUN SHIP**

Item	Ft²	
Fore course	1338	
Fore topsail	1435	
Fore topgallant sail	525	
Main course	1648	
Main topsail	1716	
Main topgallant sail	616	
Mizzen (lateen)	646	
Mizzen topsail	729	
Spritsail	448	
Jib sail	350	
Fore topmast staysail	322	
Main topmast staysail	304	
Main topgallant staysail	225	
Mizzen staysail	157.5	
Mizzen topmast staysail	136.5	
Main lower stunsail	630	(total of both 1260ft²)
Main topmast stunsail	560	(total of both 1120ft²)
Fore lower stunsail	558	(total of both 1116ft²)
Fore topmast stunsail	496	(total of both 992ft²)

TABLE 9: **SAIL SIZES**

Note
Rope sizes refer to their circumference. All the sail cloths are 2 feet in width. Any fraction contained in the dimension of a sail is divided equally between each side of it.

Sail	Cloths at		Boltropes at			
	Head	Foot	Leech	Foot	Head	Luff
Fore course	22	22	3in	3in	1¼in	–
Fore topsail	22½	14	3in	3in	1¼in	–
Fore topgallant	16	9	1½in	1½in	1in	–
Main course	26	26	3½in	3½in	1½in	–
Main topsail	27	16	3in	3in	1¼in	–
Main topgallant sail	17½	10	1¾in	1¾in	1in	–
Mizzen sail	17	17	2¾in	2¾in	1½in	–
Mizzen topsail	16	10	1½in	1½in	1in	–
Spritsail	16	16	1½in	1½in	¾in	–
Fore lower stunsail	9	9	1¼in	1¼in	1in	–
Main lower stunsail	9	9	1¼in	1¼in	1in	–
Fore topmast stunsail	9½	5	1¼in	1¼in	¾in	–
Main topmast stunsail	10½	5½	1¼in	1¼in	¾in	–
Jib sail	10	5½	1in	1in	–	1in
Fore topmast staysail	9½	5½	1¼in	1¼in	–	1¼in
Main topmast staysail	9	5½	1¼in	1¼in	–	1¼in
Main topgallant staysail	7½	5½	1in	1in	–	1in
Mizzen staysail	8½	5½	1¼in	1¼in	–	1¼in
Mizzen topmast staysail	6½	5½	1in	1in	–	1in

The pinnace generally had a breadth of between 5 feet 8 inches and 6 feet and a depth of 2 feet 6 inches. Like most naval boats she was of carvel construction and double-banked with eight oars each side. The rowlocks were cut into the gunwale thereby giving the craft greater freeboard without hindering the operation of the oars. Usually this boat was stowed in the waist of the ship, supported between the spare booms set fore and aft between the after end of the forecastle and the gallows afore the main mast. Alternatively it may have been stowed on chocks fitted on the deck in convenient positions between the hatchways. Difficulties in hoisting the boat inboard did arise. This is a

problem which appears to have been more commonplace on the smaller men-of-war. Records show that complaints concerning this were common, and some commanders preferred to have their boats towed astern.

If a yawl was carried, it can only be assumed that it was stowed inside the pinnace, for if it had been set adjacent it would have greatly restricted the deck area at the waist. Alternatively it could have been towed astern. It must have been very inconvenient if it was stowed alongside the pinnace and this may have encouraged the Navy Board to reduce the complement of boats from two to one in 1719.

In the 1660s, when introduced into naval service, the yawl was clinker-built. Though Norwegian in origin they were named after their place of manufacture, and known as Deal yawls. After about 1702 they were, like the pinnace, carvel-built, after their manufacture was transferred from the Deal boatyards to the dockyards. Most yawls were eight-oared but it seems more likely that those carried on the Sixth Rates would have been six-oared.

Whether any other type of boat was used as an alternative on 20-gun ships is a matter of speculation. If any were, it would have been purely left to the commander's discretion. The only feasible alternative would have been a longboat, which was generally replaced by pinnaces and barges over the next forty years. In most cases it would not have been practical to carry one on a Sixth Rate ship.

THE CREW

The complement of a 20-gun ship such as *Blandford* consisted of approximately 120–130 officers and men. Of this number about 25 were either of commissioned or warrant officer status, about 20 were able seamen, and approximately 70 were ordinary seamen, the remaining members of the ship's company being carpenters' mates, cooks, officers' servants and so on. The only officers who held the King's Commission were the commander and his lieutenant. The remaining officers such as the master and boatswain were of warrant officer status and held the King's Warrant. The gunner, carpenter, boatswains' mates, quartermaster and coxswain were classified as non-commissioned officers. The captain was allowed to have four servants per hundred men of the ship's company, thus on *Blandford* there were four servants and one steward.

During any action the majority of the able and ordinary seamen manned the guns, the remaining men assisting with sailing the vessel. One question that does arise concerns the number of personnel manning the sweeps. If each sweep was rowed by three men a total of 108 would have been needed. Therefore to manoeuvre the ship with sweeps while her guns were manned for action was impossible so the advantage of the hybrid vessel was lost due to the actual manpower available. The addition of a further 100 seamen to carry out such duties would have been ideal, but the costs of running and victualling a ship with approximately 230 crew would have been impractical.

SOURCES

At the Public Records Office, Kew:

Captains' Logs – Blandford

ADM 51/113	11 February 1719/20	– 12 March 1720/21
ADM 51/113	30 April 1721	– 30 April 1723
ADM 51/113	1 June 1723	– 31 December 1723
ADM 51/113	31 May 1727	– 31 October 1729
ADM 51/113	13 June 1730	– 31 December 1731
ADM 51/113	11 May 1733	– 31 December 1740
ADM 51/114	10 October 1741	– 1742

Masters Logs – Blandford

ADM 52/130	10 April 1720	– 11 January 1720/21
ADM 52/348	9 February 1720/21	– 24 November 1724
ADM 52/348	13 May 1727	– 20 January 1729/30
ADM 52/349	21 January 1729/30	– 2 August 1732
ADM 52/349	11 May 1733	– 9 January 1737/38
ADM 52/546	12 February 1741/42	– 29 September 1742

Ship Muster Books for the Blandford

ADM 36/217	1727
ADM 36/219	1727–28
ADM 36/218	1728
ADM 36/221	1728–29
ADM 36/222	1729–30
ADM 36/223	1730–31
ADM 36/224	1731–32
ADM 36/225	1735–36
ADM 36/226	1736–37
ADM 36/227	1737–39
ADM 36/220	1739–40
ADM 36/228	1739–51
ADM 36/230	1741–42
ADM 36/252	1741–46
ADM 36/231	1742–43

Sources for the tables

Table 1: *Naval Administration 1715–1750*, Navy Records Society, Vol 120; Progress Books Vols I and II, NMM, and Dimension Book B, NMM, except for column 5, the information in which was extracted from a letter from the Navy Board to the Admiralty Secretary dated 18 February 1716/17.

Table 2: Costs for a 24- and 20-gun ship, PRO Adm 1/5114/17; costs for a 20-gun ship, NMM SPB 37a ms61/030 and *Shipwright's Notebook 1720–1760*, by William Wilkins; costs of figurehead and ornamentation, NMM SPB 20 ms9355 and extracts from *Shipwright's Notebook*.

Table 3: Progress Books Vols I and II, NMM.

Table 4: *Shipbuilding Unveiled*, 1717, by William Sutherland.

Table 6: 1719 Establishment Book, PRO Adm 170/429.

BIBLIOGRAPHY

Anderson, R C *Oared Fighting Ships*, Marshall, 1962

Baugh, D A *Naval Administration 1715–1750*, Vol 120, Navy Records Society

Blackmore, H L *The Armouries of the Tower of London*, HMSO, 1976

Goodwin, P *The Construction and Fitting of the Sailing Man of War 1650–1850*, Conway Maritime Press, 1987

Howard, Dr F *Sailing Ships of War 1400–1860*, Conway Maritime Press, 1979

Lavery, B *Deane's Doctrine of Naval Architecture 1670*, Conway Maritime Press, 1981

Lavery, B *Ship of the Line*, 2 vols, Conway Maritime Press, 1983–84

Lees, J *The Masting and Rigging of English Ships of War 1625–1860*, Conway Maritime Press, 1979

May, Cdr W E *Boats of Men of War*, NMM Publication

Ranft, B McI *The Vernon Papers* Vol XCIX, Navy Records Society

Sutherland, W *Englands Glory* or *Shipbuilding Unveiled*, 1717

1719 Establishment Book

Progress Book Vols 1 and 2

Dimension Book B

APPENDIX: THE DIMENSIONS AUTHORISED FOR THE 20-GUN SHIPS OF THE 1719 ESTABLISHMENT

		Ft	In
Length of the Keel for Tonnage		87	9
Length of the Gundeck from the Rabbet of the Stem to the Rabbet of the Post		106	0
Breadth, Extreme		28	4
Breadth at the after part of the Main Transom from out to outside of the Plank		16	2
Breadth at the Toptimber Line out to out	Afore	–	–
	Midships	22	10
	Abaft	13	0
Breadth of the Stern at the Fiferaile abaft		11	9
Height of the Cutting Down in the Dead Flat above the Keel		1	4
Height of the Toptimber line or Upper edge of the Waist Raile above the Bottom of the False Keel	Afore	23	4
	Midships	21	4
	Abaft	26	5
Rising of the Midships Flat		–	10
Depth in the Hold taken from the Strake next the Limberboards		9	2
Strake next the Limberboard	Thick		5
	Broad (if can be had)	1	0
Burthen in Tunns		374	87/94
Draught of Water	Afore	11	4
	Abaft	12	4
Platform			
Abaft, height between Plank to Plank (at the Middle of the Beams)		5	7
Afore, height between Plank to Plank (at the Middle of the beam)		5	7

Lower Deck
		Ft	In
Beams to Round			3
Plank, Thick			2
Height to the Upper Edge of the Quarter Deck Beams at the middle of the Beam (Afore, Midships, Abaft)		5	9
Height, to the Sweep Port Cills from the Waterline Midships		2	7
Height, to the Ballast Port Cill from the Waterline Midships		2	7

Upper or Main Deck
		Ft	In
Beams to Round			6
Plank, Thick			2
Height to the Upper Edge of the Quarter Deck Beams at the middle of the Beams	Afore	6	5
	Abaft	6	6
Height to the Upper Edge of the Forecastle Beams at the middle of the Beams, Afore and Abaft		4	8
Gunports	Deep		
	Broad		

Forecastle
		Ft	In
Beams to Round			5
Plank, Thick			2
Length from the fore side of the Planking		7	3

Quarterdeck
		Ft	In
Beams to Round			6
Plank, Thick			2
Length, taken midships from the after part of the Counter Timbers		16	9
Length, from the fore side of the Tafferaile at the Height of the Fiferaile to the fore side of the Figure of the Head at a line parallel to the Keel		121	11
Rounding of the Stern, at the Wing Transom (not applicable to those vessels built with the Square Tuck)			6
Rounding of the Stern, at the Lower Counter			8
Gundeck (Upper or Main deck) perpendicular height above the Upper Edge of the Keel, to the upper edge of the Plank at the middle line of the Deck	Afore		
	Abaft		
The Back of the False Post to Rake Two and a Half inches in a Foot and the upright of the Stern, three inches			
The Stem to Rake Forward above the Lower Deck to the top of it One Inch in a Foot			
The Height of the Upper edge of the Wing Transom above the Upper edge of the Keel at the Post		15	6½
Lower Height of the Breadth above the Upper edge of the Keel in the Dead Flat		10	5
Upper Height of the Breadth above the Upper edge of the Keel in the Dead Flat		11	5
From the Upper edge of the Keel to the Lower edge of the Counter Raile at the middle line		18	0
From the After side of the Wing Transom to the After part of the Counter at the middle line		3	4
From the Upper edge of the Keel to the Lower edge to the Lower edge of the Raile under the Great Cabbin Lights			

Parts of the Frame
	Ft	In
Keel, Main of Elm or Beach, No of Pieces not to be exceeded, 4		
Square in the Midships	1	0
Scarphs, (laid with Tarr and Hair), Thrice their Breadth or;	3	4
Number and Size of Bolts; 6 of ⅞ in dia		
Keel, Sided afore		10½
Sided at the Rabbet of the Post		7½
False Keel, Thick		3
Number of Pieces; The Same or One more than the Main Keel		
Stem, Main, Breadth at the Head athwartships	1	2
Below the Hance; The Bigness of the Keel amidships		
Fore and Aft at the Head	1	0
At the Fore foot; The same as the Keel		
Scarphs, not less than	3	0
No and Size of Bolts in each and to go through the False Stem; 6 of ⅞ in dia		
False Stem (or Apron) Thick, (to overlaunch the Scarphs of the Stem, above and below)		6
Broad, (if can be had)	1	6
Scarphs, long	1	0
Post, Main, Square at the Upper End, the Top to be wrought upwards if can be had	1	0
Fore and Aft on the Keel, the False Post included	2	0
Abaft the Rabbet at the Wing Transom		5½
False, the back of it Abaft the Rabbet of the Keel	1	5
The Inner, Fore and Aft, (the Top end upward)		8
Fore and Aft on the Keel, (if to be had)		9
Transoms, Wing sided		10½
Moulded at the ends	1	0
Deck, to lye close to the Lower Deck for the Plank of the said Deck to Bolt into the same		
Sided		8½
Moulded, as Broad as conveniently may be for the Better fastening the Plank of the Deck		
Between the Wing Transom and Deck, so thick as to leave 2 inches between the Wing Transom and the Lower Deck Planking for the circulation of Air		
[The earlier built 20-gun ships were constructed with a square tuck, so no other transoms were fitted below the deck transom of the lower deck. However, later vessels had a round tuck stern. In this case a further three transoms were fitted below the lower deck transom. The moulding of each of these transoms is given as 7½ inches with spaces of no less than 3 inches for air circulation between them.]		
Rising Wood, A sufficient number of pieces, Afore and Abaft		
Abaft, (if a short piece of Keel) to overlaunch the Scarph at least 6 feet, if a Long piece of Keel to drop short of the Scarph 8 feet		
Depth in the Midships on the Keel		7
Broad, in the Midships 3 inches on each side of the Keel, (if can be had)		
Knee, against the Post, upon the Lower piece of Deadwood, Length of the Up and Down Arm	4	0
Fore and Aft Arm, (if can be had)	5	0
Distance and Size of Bolts; Spaced every 22 inches, diameter being 1 in. Bolted through the Keel and Post, and upon the said Knee to bring on the rest of the Rising Wood fastened in the same manner		

Hawsepieces, No on each side, Two, and a piece between, or Four as conveniently be had			
If in Two, each piece to be Broad		2	0
Hawse Holes, Diameter			9½

Timbers

Room and Space		2	5
Floor and Foothook and the Bearing of the Ship to fill up the Rooms and Space			
Next the Flats, Sided			9
Afore and Abaft, In wake of the Half Timbers, One inch less			
At the Wrongheads, Dead Flat, wrought in and out			7
Afore and Abaft, in and out			6
Every other bolted through the Keel by bolts of 1in dia			
Heads to lye above the Bearing of the Floor		1	4
Foothooks, Lower sided in the Dead Flat next the Flats a small distance afore and abaft the Bearing of the Ship			9
Afore and abaft, that stated above			8
Heel to Scarph below the Floorheads, at least		5	6
In and out at the Heads in the Dead Flat			5½
Scarphs, upwards long		5	4
afore and abaft, not less than		5	0
Foothooks, Second, sided in the Midships			8½
Afore and abaft, sided			7½
Scarphs long in the Dead Flat		5	4
Afore and abaft, not less than		5	0
Foothooks, Upper, sided in the Dead Flat			8
sided afore and abaft			7½
[Both stated above were to be 1 inch less at their Heads]			
In and out at the Lower Deck in the Dead Flat			5
Scarphs, Long, in the Midships		5	4
Upper and Lower, afore and abaft		5	0
Top, sided at the Heels and at the Upper Foothook Heads			8
Sided at the Heads			6
In and Out at the Gunnell or Top of the Sides			2¼
To be placed in wake of the Channells, some on each side if can be had			

In (the) Hold

Keelson, Square			11½
Number of pieces if can be had; 4			
Length of the Scarphs to reach Three Floor Timbers and to be bolted with Bolts of the same size of the Floor Timbers, and Two Bolts in the Ends of the Scarphs			
Standard, upon or under the Keelson abaft, the Up and Down Arme to Butt under the Lower Transom if can be had			
The other Arme Long		7	0
Sided, at least			10
Limberboards	Thick		2
	Broad	1	0
Thickstuff at the Floorheads. Middle Strake,	Thick		5
	Broad, if can be had	1	1½
Thickness of the Strakes above and below the Middle Strake			3
Number of Strakes above and below the Middle Strake; 1			
No more than One Strake of 2½ inches in thickness afore or abaft, fitted in 20 Gun ships			
Thickstuff at the Lower Foothook Heads. Middle Strake	Thick		3¼
	Broad	1	0
Strake both above and below the Middle Strake, Thick			2
Footwaling (in this case also applies to the Strake next the Limber Boards)			
Thick, in the Midships			2
Afore and abaft			1¾
Platform Clamps, Not fitted [the Beams for the Platforms were probably Bolted down upon the Thickstuff over the Lower Foothook Heads]			
Platform Planking, [The deck planking was mainly made up of Boards 2 inches thick and where no loading was required (*ie* the wings outboard of the magazine) possibly made of 1½–1¾ Boards]			
Crotches, Number fitted; one			
Length of each Arme (if can be had)		5	0
Sided			8
Number of bolts of ¾ inches Diameter, fitted; 6			
Steps Main, sided – The Diameter of the Mainmast in the Partners			
Deep on the Keelson		1	0
Fore, sided – To the Diameter of the Foremast in the Partners			
On the Keelson, – A sufficient depth			
Length (if can be had)		7	0
Both the Main and the Fore Mast Steps were fastened with Six Bolts of 1 inch Diameter			
Mizen, sided – To the Diameter of the Mizenmast in the Partners			
On the Keelson, – A sufficient Depth			
Fastened with Six Bolts of ¾ inch in diameter			
Main Capstan (if fitted in this form) Step,	Broad	1	3
	Deep	1	0
Breast Hooks, One fitted below the Lower Deck Hook, sided; Two fitted of the same Siding forming the Step for the Foremast			9
Pillars, Upright under the (Lower Deck) Beams, Square			5
To be placed under the Middle of each Beam and in the Quarters on the Scarphs of the Riders [not generally fitted on initial Building unless a Rebuild or later modification to 'stiffen' the Hull]			
Well, Fore and Aft		6	0
Thwartships		5	8
Planking, Thick			2
Shot Lockers, One only, fitted abaft the Well			
Fore and aft in the Clear		1	10
Plank, Thick, (integral with that of the Well)			2
Bulkheads, Length from the Inside of the Rabbet of the Stern Post on the Lower Deck to the After side of the Magazine [this dimension may have varied between the first Building Programme and the Third.]		18	6

Lower Deck

Clamps, In two Strakes. Upper	Thick		4
	Broad	1	2
Lower	Thick	1	1
	Broad	3	0
Lengths of the Scarphs		3	0
Openings under them			8
Breast (deck) Hook and Hook under the Hawses	sided		9
	Length	12	0
Number of ¾ inch diameter Bolts, 9			
Breast Hook, under the Lower Deck (Deck Hook) to have a Large Chock and to be left as much as possible fore and aft for the Better Coaking, Bolting and Fastening the Planks of the Lower Deck to the Same			
Beams, sided in the Midships (One inch less afore and abaft each way)			8
Moulded in the Midships (One inch less afore and abaft each way)			7
One to be placed under and one between each Port where conveniently be had except in the Wake of the Hatchways and Masts and there to have Doubled Armed Beams, that one part may be proper Standards where necessary and double Kneed at each end with One Hanging Knee and One Lodging Knee. [Standards were employed towards the fore and After ends due to the acute shape of the Hull below the waterline at these points]			
Knees, Sided,	Lodging		5½
	Hanging		6
Those (of the above stated) in Wake of the Main and Fore Masts and Main Hatch, to be ½ an inch bigger			
Hanging Arm Long (if can be had)		4	6
Lodging Arme to the Beam, Long		3	0
Hanging Knees to be Bolted with 6 Bolts of ¾ inches diameter			
To have 4 Bolts in the lower arms of the Hanging Knees, especially in Wake of the Masts and Hatchways and where the Knees can be got of sufficient length			
Carlings, Number of Tires (tiers) on each side; 2	Broad		5½
	Deep		4½
Ledges, to lye asunder not less than 9 inches, not more than 12	Broad		3
	Deep		2½
Bitts (Riding), Number of Pairs; 1½ [However, this was not always the case for often the fore set consisted of two separate halves, the cross piece tying both being omitted because of the postion of the fore mast]			
The Foremost fitted – as conveniently as possible			
The Aftermost to be abaft the Rabbet of the Stem		26	0
Distance between them, Thwartships	Foremost		
	Aftermost		
Aftermost	Square	1	1
Foremost	Square		11
Crosspieces, Foremost (if fitted)	Deep		11
	Fore and Aft	1	2
Length, as conveniently be got			
Lower Edge above the Deck		1	4
Scored in Deep			2
Elme Back of; Thick			4
Aftermost, Deep			11
Fore and Aft		1	2

Length, as conveniently be got			
Lower Edge above the Deck		1	3
Scored in Deep			2
Elme Back of, Thick			4
Standard Knees (for the After Bitts), sided			9
To be Sufficiently Deep to make the Carling if can be had			
The Arme upon the deck to be as long as the Bitt pins are asunder and the Forepart to be Flush with the Deck			
To be Bolted with 4 Bolts of 1 inch diameter			
Waterway, Thick, in the Chine; One inch thicker than the Plank of the Deck			
Plank, on the Flat to be English, in the Wake of the Standards. Thick;			1
Two Strakes next the Coamings to be one Inch thicker than the rest of the Deck and to be let down an Inch on the Beams, to be bolted with 2 Small Bolts in each Beam and One Treenail in each Ledge, the size of the Bolts to be ½ an Inch and to be 1 inch longer than Twice the Thickness of the Plank. All the rest of the Plank to be Bolted with one Bolt in each Beam and one Treenaile on each Ledge			
Partners, for the Masts, Main to be Carlings	Broad		11
	Deep	1	0
Fore, Thick			4
Mizen, No thicker than the Deck			
Bowsprit, Thick			5
Main Capstan, Thick			5
Step for the Main Capstan, Thick		1	0
To be no higher above the Deck than 4 inches if it can be done			
Transom Knees, The Wing sided			7
The fore and aft Arme to be scored into the Timbers 1½ inches and to Scarph with Hook and Butt at the Fore end on the Spirketting a sufficient Length			
Fore and Aft Arme, Long (if can be had)		10	0
Shortest Arme, Long (if can be had)		6	0
Bolted with bolts of ¾ inches diameter set every 24 inches apart			
Deck, sided, the same as that of the Hanging Knees			
Length of the Longest Arme		6	0
Distance and size of the Bolts the same as the Wing Transom Knees			
Below the Lower Deck, sided 2 inches less than the Wing Transom Knees			
Length of the Longest Arme		6	0
Distance and size of the Bolts, the same as the Wing Transom			
Hatches, Main	Fore and Aft	5	0
	Thwartships	4	0
Fore	Fore and Aft		
	Thwartships		
Next abaft the Mainmast	Fore and Aft		
	Thwartships		
Over the Fishroom	Fore and Aft		
	Thwartships		
Plank for Ditto, Thick; One and a Half inches for each			
Height above the Deck			2
Scuppers, Lead, number on each side being Three with a diameter of 4 inches [Additional Scuppers were sited forward of the Manger]			
Manger, Plank Thick			
Scuppers, number on each side being Two of 4 inches in diameter			
Pump Dale Scupper, Diameter in the Clear			6
Spirketting, Two Strakes on each side to be bolted in the next Timber to each Butt with One Bolt			
Thickness in the Midships	The Lower Edge		3
	The Upper Edge		2½
Plank, between the Spirketting and the Upper Deck Clamps, Thick			2
Ports, In the Counter, Number; 2			
Oar Ports, Number; 36			
	Depth		8
	Fore and Aft		7½
Ballast [Port], Number; 1			
	Depth		
	Fore and Aft		
Pillars, Turned Square			4½
Tiller, Square in the Biggest end			8
Sweep, to be flush with the Beam	Thickness		2
	Broad		6¼
Transom, Deep			7
Transom Knees, Deep			6
Transom Knees, Armes, fore and aft, long if can be had		7	6
Thwartships		3	8
To be fastened with same size and number of bolts as used for the Upper Deck Knees			

Upper Deck (Main Deck)

Clamps, to be wrought Anchor Stock Fashion with Hook and Butt			
Thick at the Upper edge			3
Thick at the Lower edge			2½
Beams, Sided			8½
Moulded			6½
To lye One under and One between each Port, where they can conveniently be placed, and as near as possible over the Beams of the Lower Deck and under the Great Cabbin the Distance of the others			
Knees, Double at each End, Hanging and Lodging, Sided			5
The Up and Down Arme to reach the Spirketting			
Shortest Arme, Long, if can be had		2	10
To be fastened with Five Bolts of ⅝ inches diameter			
Carlings	Broad		6
	Deep		4½
Number of Tire (Tier) on each side except in Wake of the Hatchways and Mainmast; 2			
Short, with Long Coamings of Oake on them, pricked down One Inch into the Beams			
Coamings to lye above the Deck			3
Broad, with the Rabbet			8½
Ledges	Broad		3¼
	Deep		3
To lye Asunder, From 9 to 12 inches			
Waterway, Thick on the Chine; One inch more than the Flat of the Deck			
Partners, for the Foremast, Thick			5
Mainmast – see Carlings, [but was more probably, Thick			5]
Mizenmast, Thick			3½
Flats, Three Strakes next the Waterways and all the Forepart of the Deck to be of Oake, Thick			2
Two Strakes of Oake next the Coamings to give scarph to each other and to be pricked down an Inch into the Beams, Tyld (tailed) and hooked into the Transom and Deckhook and bolted to the Beams, Breasthook and Transom. The rest to be of Prutia (Prussia) Deal			
[Capstans – see drawings as no details are listed for the 20-gun ship]			
Spirketting, Two Strakes on each side			
Thickness at the Lower Edge	Lower Strake		2½
	Upper Strake		2
Scuppers, Lead, on each Side, Number			6
Diameter in the Clear			4½
Standards of Iron, One Pair			
The up and down arm to reach the Upper Edge and Bolt thro' the Forecastle and Quarter Deck Clamps. [This contradicts the previous statement as only One pair fitted. On inspection of existing models Iron Standards are omitted therefore leaving doubt as to their actual application]			
If Fitted – Shortest Arme, Long		2	11
Fastened with Five Bolts of ⅝ inches diameter			
Stringer in the Waist, made integral with the Planksheer			
Bitts, Main Topsaile Sheet and Jeer, Square			7
Jeer, high above the Deck		3	2
Sheet and Jeer Crosspieces	Fore and Aft		6
	Deep		5
	Scored into the Bitts		1½
Crosspiece of the Gallows, (if fitted)	Sided		6½
	Deep		11
	Long	9	0
Upper edge above the Deck		6	0
Scored in			1½
Bolts, Ring and Eye for the Ports, Four in number per port, ¾ inches diameter			
Diameter of the Rings in the Clear			4
On the Flat of the Deck for the Guns, Size			¾
Eye for lashing the Blocks on each side of the Mainmast and the Foremast, Size			¾
Ditto, for the Toptackles, diameter			1¼
All Carlings and Ledges afore and abaft where they are Shorter to be made lesser than in the Midships			
Bitts, Fore Topsaile Sheet, Squire; (to meet in the Middle)*			6
Jeer, Square; (to meet in the Middle)*			6
High above the Deck		3	2
Crosspieces	Fore and Aft		6
	Deep		5
	Scored into the Bitts		1½
Bolts, Span Shackle, (the corner of the Shackle to be Round), Size			1¼
Number fitted; Two			
Eye for the Main Topmast Stay; ⅞ inches diameter			

* The Bitts were more commonly fitted separately and did not marry in the middle at the Deck

Quarterdeck		
Clamps, Upper edge, Thick		3
Lower edge, Thick		2
String of Oake in the Great Cabbin, Upper edge, Thick		2½
Lower edge, Thick		2
Broad, if can be had	1	0
Beams, To have a Small Strap of Iron round the Timber to every Second and Third Beam in Wake of the Cabbin		
Sided		5½
Moulded		4½
To lye asunder from 2 feet 4 inches to 2 feet each where they can be conveniently placed		
In the Great Cabbin, to be Bolted into the Strings at their ends with Bolts of; ⅝ inch diameter		
Knees, Hanging, Sided		4
[These were not generally fitted. If, however, they were the up and down arm would have been worked down to the spirketting, the short arm being approximately 2 feet 4 inches in length. The knees would be fastened with bolts of ⅝ inch diameter]		
Waterways, Thick on the Chine; One Inch thicker than the Plank of the Deck		
Spirketting, Thick		2
Quickwork, berthed up with Deale, thick		1½
Gunnell to the Taffarell, Deep		3
Forecastle		
Clamps, Thick		2½
Broad [this dimension is illegible in the Establishment Book, so it has been estimated]	1	1
Beams, Sided		4
Moulded		3
Asunder	2	0
Knees, Hanging, (if fitted to the aftermost Beam), Sided		4
The up and down Arm to reach the Spirketting		
The Shortest Arm, Long	2	3
Fastened with 5 Bolts of ⅝ inch diameter		
Waterways, Thick in the Chine; One inch thicker than the Deck		
Beam at the Fore part of the Forecastle to fasten the Cathead		
Broad or Double	1	2
Deep (under the Rabbet of the Deck)		5
Catheads, Square		9
Eye, for the Main Topmast Stay; ⅞ inches diameter		
Without Board		
Wales, Main and Stuff between to be an equal Thickness, to be wrought with Hook and Butt		
Deep from the Upper to Lower Edge	2	6
Thick		4
One Strake above them, Thick		3
Strake below the Wales (Diminishing Strake) number fitted 1		
Thickness at the Upper Edge		3
Thickness at the Lower Edge		2½
The Rest of the Plank under the Thickstuff to be Wrought full to these Thicknesses at the Floorhead		2½
Deal, in the Waist, at the Top of the Side, Thick		2
Channels, Main, Length (if the Ports will admit)	17	6
Breadth, at the Foremost End (However, must be sufficient to Carry the Shrouds clear of the Gunnell and the Fiferails)	1	7
Thickness, at the Inner Edge		4
Thickness, at the Outer Edge		2¾
Fastened with 5 bolts of ¾ inches diameter		
Fore, Length (if the Ports will admit)	15	0
Breadth, at the After End	1	4
(However must be sufficient to Carry the Shrouds clear of the Gunnels)		
Thickness at the Inner Edge		4
Thickness at the Outer Edge		2¾
Fastened with 5 bolts of ¾ inches diameter		
Mizen, Length	7	6
Breadth (However must be sufficient to Carry the Shrouds clear of the Gunnell and the Fiferail)	1	1
Thickness at the Inner Edge		2½
Thickness at the Outer Edge		1¾
Fastened with 3 bolts of ½ inch diameter)		
Chain Plates, Main and Fore, Broad		2¼
Thick in the middle		⅞
Thick at the Edges		½
Size of the Bolts		1⅛
Mizen, Broad		1¾
Thick in the middle		⅝

Thick at the edges		⅜
Size of bolts		1⅛
Plates, Ring and Backstay for the Main Chaines to have the same Breadth and Thickness and the same size Bolts as the Main Chains		
Bindings for the Deadeyes for the Main and Fore Channells, their size		1⅛
Bindings for the Deadeyes for the Mizen Channell, their size		¾
Deadeyes, for the Main Channells, number fitted including One Spare; 6		
Diameter		11
For the Fore Channells, Number fitted including One Spare; 5		
Diameter		10
Main and Fore Channells to be in Thickness ¾ of an inch or more than Half the Diameter		
For the Mizen Channells, Number fitted; 3		
Diameter		7
To be in Thickness ½ an Inch more than Half the Diameter		
For the Main Topmast Backstays, Two of 7 inches diameter (each side)		
For the Main Topgallant Backstays, One of 5 inches diameter (each side)		
For the Foretopmast Backstays, Two of 6 inches diameter (each side)		
For the Fore Topgallant Backstays, One of 5 inches diameter (each side)		
For the Mizen Topmast Backstay, One of 5 inches diameter (each side)		
Rother, Head, Thwartships (if can conveniently be had)	1	1
Fore and Aft (if can conveniently be had)	1	3
At the Lower end, Fore and Aft, One Tenth part of the Ships Extreme Breadth		
Braces and Pintles, Number of Pair; 5		
Upper afore the Rabbet of the Post, Long	2	6
Lower afore the Back of the Post, Long	4	0
To be Hung Flemish Fashion, and secured with Chocks above the Water to prevent its unhanging		
Pintles, Diameter		2
Length of the Upper Pintles		9
Length of the Lower Pintle only to be		11
Braces and Straps for Pintles, Broad		3
Thick in the Shoulder at the Return		1⅛
To have an Iron Strap on the Back and on each Corner an Eye well Clenched on the side of the Strap, of Sufficient Bigness to receive an Ovall Ring		
Head, The Knee to be as Thick as the Stem		
Size of the Two upper Bolts in the Knee		1⅜
Size of the Two upper Bolts in the Stem		1¼
Cheeks, Sided if can conveniently be had, Lower		7
Upper		6
Length of the Arm next the Side (if can be had) The Bolts the same size as the Lower Deck knees	6	6
Timbers, Sided from		4 to 3
Length from the Fore side of the Stem to the Fore part of the Knee of the Head	7	0
Standard in the Head, sided; (bolted as the Lower Deck knees)		7½
Upper Rails at the after end, Fore and Aft		7
Thwartships		5¼
Chesstrees, sided at the Gunwale		4½
Fenders, sided at the Gunwale		2½
against the Hatchways, Asunder	1	4
Linings of the Anchors, Thick		2
Rails on the Side, the Sheer, Broad		5½
Thick		2¼
Waist Rail, Broad		5½
Thick (dimension unknown, no planshere)		
After Drift, Broad		4
Thick		2½
Fife Rail, Broad		8
Thick		2½
Drifts, Thick		2
To be Struck with an Astricall within and without, and the Square to overhang the Plank or Deal Half an Inch within and without Board		
Shankpainter Chain, Long	10	6
Size of the Links		¾
Port Hinges [no dimensions given]		
Bolts, for the Butt ends under water where they are necessary to be placed in the Timber next the Butt and to be Clenched within side, Size (Diameter)		¾
Eye for the Standing part of the Main and Fore Sheats, Size		1⅛
for the Mizen Sheat, Main Brace, Main and Fore Topsaile Halyards, Bowsprit Shrouds and in Wake of the Chain Plates, Size		1
for the Mizen Topsaile Halyard and the Mizen Truss, size		¾
Swivle, for the Longboat, size		1
Diameter of the Ring in the clear		2¾
Lining of the Hawse, between the Holes, Thick		5
Bolt Holes to be bored through, size		⅝

The Photographs

3. Overall view of a 20-gun ship *c*1719. This Science Museum model has two features that demonstrate the evolution of this type. It is fitted with quarter galleries that replaced the earlier quarter badges, and features the square beakhead bulkhead which replaced the round bow.
Science Museum

4. Model, *c*1730 of a 20-gun ship which was never actually built. It illustrates clearly the modifications made to 20-gun ships of the 1719 Establishment. The quarterdeck has been extended forward and the steering wheel raised from the upper deck to the quarterdeck. The aftermost gunport is shown here as a light for the after cabin, thus only ten guns were fitted each side. A second set of gallows is fitted for boat stowage.
National Maritime Museum

5. View of port quarter of a 20-gun ship, *c*1725 showing the quarter gallery which was introduced to these vessels to replace the quarter badge lights. Other features of interest are the square tuck transom and the unusual moulded arch fitted over the middle gunport. Although at this period the quarterdeck had been extended forward, the forecastle was still short, finishing afore the fore mast. Note that the steering wheel has been raised to the quarterdeck from its original position on the upper deck.
National Maritime Museum

6. Stern view of a 20-gun ship with a small square tuck transom. This model also shows that despite the introduction of the quarter galleries, there were still five stern counter timbers. This suggests that little alteration was necessary in replacing the quarter badge lights with quarter galleries. The main features of the decoration can be seen.
Science Museum

7. Stern view of a model, *c*1730. Although not executed with the skill of a good craftsman, it shows the general features of the decoration at this period. Note that the model has the round tuck stern standard on larger ships of the period.
National Maritime Museum

8. *Tartar*, a 20-gun ship, *c*1734. She was 'rebuilt' from a 32-gun ship of the same name built in 1702. This is one of the earliest models rigged with sails, and clearly shows the driver (a sail that was introduced to replace the lateen) abaft the mizzen mast. Note the absence of the oar ports and the manner in which the pinnace was stowed in the waist of the ship on spare spars.
National Maritime Museum

9. View of the port bow of a 20-gun ship, *c*1730 showing the typical round bow of the first generation of these ships. The figurehead and head rails are clearly shown but lack the finish of a skilled craftsman.
National Maritime Museum

10. and 11. Model of the 20-gun ship *Lowestoffe*, showing the layout of the deck beams, carlings, and ledges. **10.** View looking forward. Note the roundhouses built integral with the hull planking and the seats of ease fitted within them. The square hole forward of the foremost hatch is for the galley flue (which is missing on the model because it was badly damaged). **11.** Quarterdeck and after section of the upper deck. A typical feature of these vessels was that the doorway to the captain's quarter was always situated on the port side.
National Maritime Museum

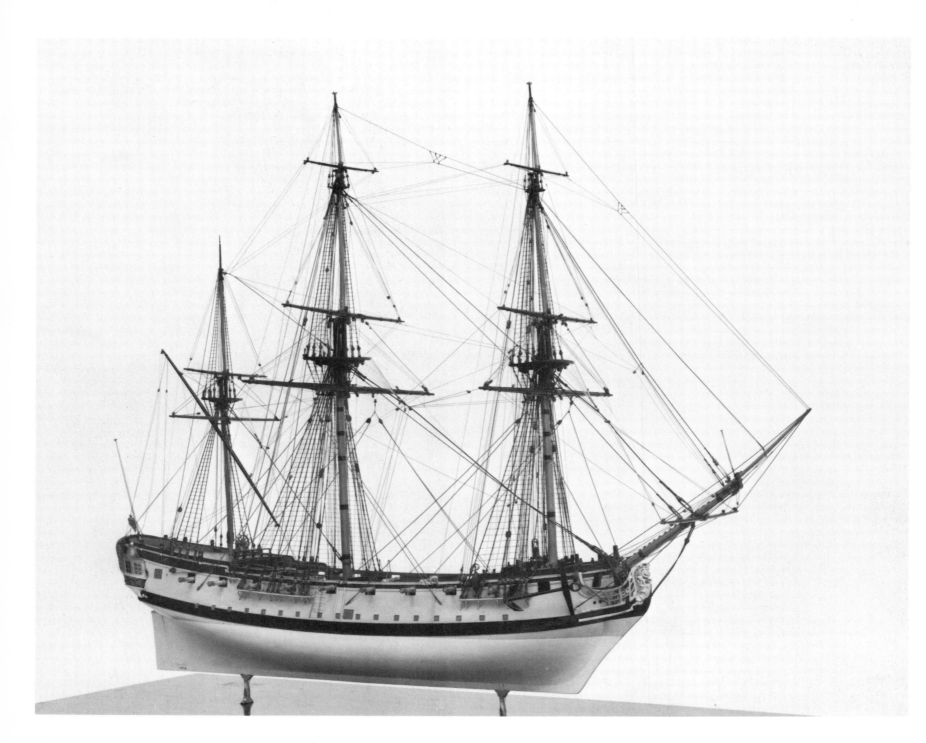

12. Model of a 20-gun ship, *c*1730. The rigging is contemporary. The model is a fair representation but does not have the finish of a skilled craftsman.
National Maritime Museum

13. The decoration of the stern of a 20-gun ship, showing details of the counters and taffarel. National Maritime Museum model. *Author*

14. The fore channel and head of a National Maritime Museum model of a 20-gun ship, showing the manner in which the bower, sheet and kedge anchors were stowed. Note the main course tack which is coiled and secured to the shrouds. *Author*

15. The decoration of the quarter badge, quarter figure on a model of a 20-gun ship at the National Maritime Museum. *Author*

The Drawings

Plans used for the drawings

Blandford, Lyme, Scarborough	3074 & 3074A, Box 43	NMM
Bideford	2939 & 2939A, Box 45	NMM
Dolphin	2797 Box 43	NMM
Garland	2757 Box 43	NMM

A General arrangements

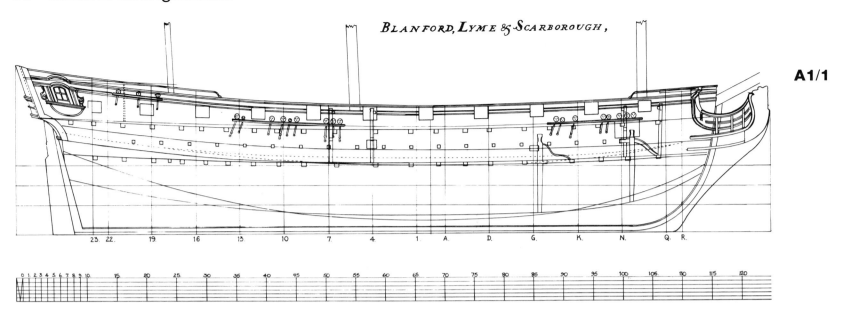

BLANFORD, LYME & SCARBOROUGH,

A1/1

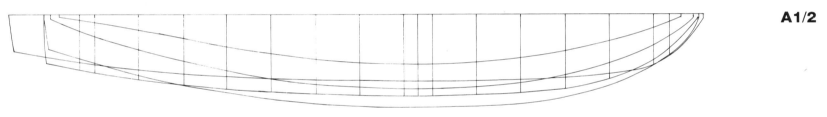

A1/2

A1 **SHEER AND HALF-BREADTH
PLAN OF *BLANDFORD*, *LYME*
AND *SCARBOROUGH* (1/192
scale)**

A1/1 **Sheer elevation**

A1/2 **Half-breadth plan**

A2 **BODY PLAN (1/96 scale)**

A2

B Hull construction

B1 **BOW**

B1/1 **Stempost and surrounding area, profile (1/48 scale)**

B1/2 **End view of stem post (1/48 scale)**
1. Stem post
2. False post or apron
3. Line of the rabbet
4. Upper deck
5. Deck hook
6. Mortice for the bowsprit heel tenon
7. Upper deck beam
8. Bowsprit step
9. Breast hook
10. Lower deck
11. Deck hook
12. Lower deck beams
13. Breast hook
14. Stemson
15. Knee of the head
16. Forward bulkhead of the galley
17. Breast hook integral with mast step
18. Fore platform deck
19. Fore mast step
20. Mortice for mast heel tenon
21. Centre line pillar
22. Keelson
23. Deadwood or rising wood
24. Hog or rising wood
25. Rabbet of the keel
26. Keel
27. False keel
28. Boxing
29. Gripe

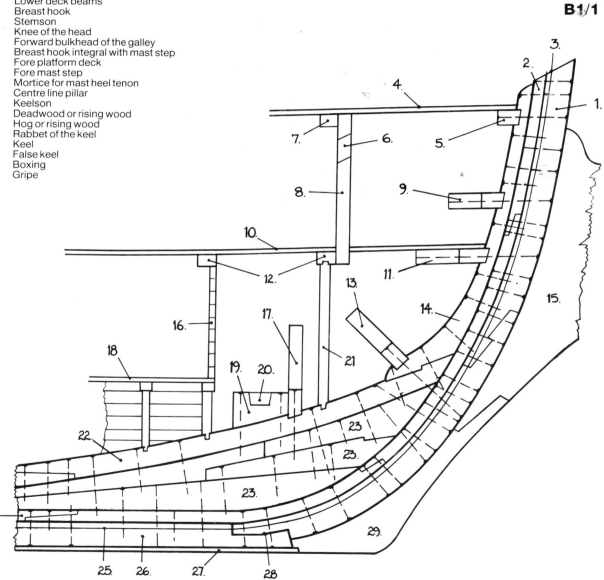

B1/1

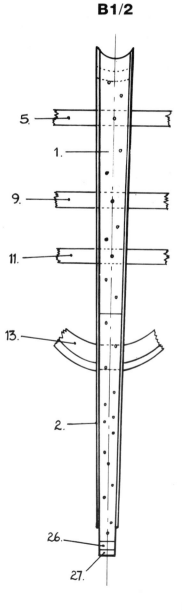

B1/2

B1/3

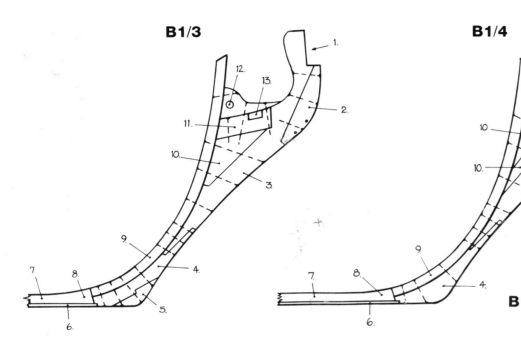

B1/4

B1/5

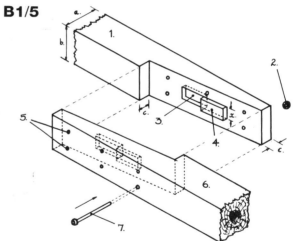

B1/6   B1/7

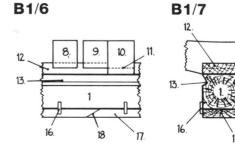

B2/1

B2/2

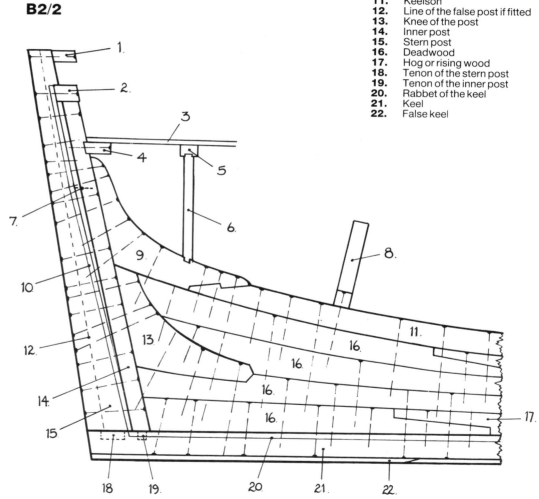

B3 FRAMING AND PLANKING

B3/1 Frames and hawse pieces in the fore body (1/96 scale)

1. Sheave block
2. Gunport sill
3. Planksheer rail
4. Sheave block
5. Sweep ports
6. Capping over the timberheads
7. Sheave block
8. Gunport lintel
9. Fife rail
10. Filling frames
11. Hawse pieces
12. Hawse holes
13. Stem post
14. Foremost square frame
15. Deadwood and apron
16. First futtock of filling frame
17. Floor timber of filling frame
18. Joint line of main frame
19. Toptimber
20. Second futtock of main frame
21. Floor timber of main frame
22. First futtock of main frame
23. Third futtock of main frame
24. Lengthening piece
25. False keel
26. Keel

B3/1

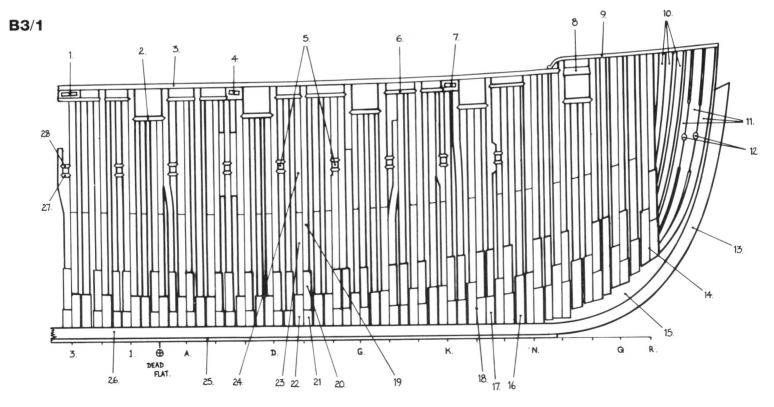

B Hull construction

B3/2 Main and filling frames in the after body (1/96 scale)

1. Quarter badge light
2. Gunport lintel
3. Gunport sill
4. Sheave block
5. Toptimber of a main frame
6. Lengthening piece of a main frame
7. Planksheer rail
8. Capping over the timberheads
9. Sweep ports
10. Timber block incorporating chain pump scupper
11. Ballast port
12. Sheave block
13. Sweep port lintel
14. Sweep port sill
15. Floor timber of a filling frame
16. Joint line of main frame
17. First futtock of filling frame
18. Third futtock of main frame
19. First futtock of main frame
20. Floor timber of main frame
21. Second futtock of main frame
22. False keel
23. Keel
24. Deadwood
25. Inner post
26. Stern post
27. Transom frame
28. Wing transom
29. Counter timber

B3/2

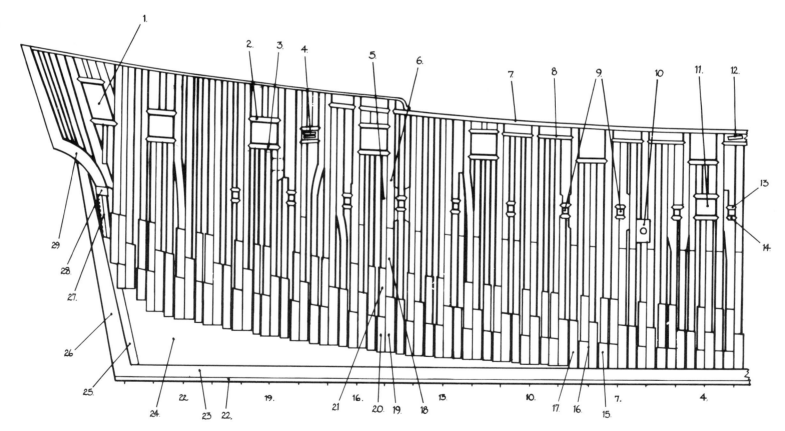

40

**B3/3 Isometric of the midship timbers
(1/64 scale)**

1. Planksheer rail
2. Sheer rail
3. Side cast lengthening piece
4. Upper deck lining (or quickwork)
5. Upper deck spirketting
6. Gunport sill
7. Timber capping piece
8. Waterway
9. Ship's side hull planking
10. Upper deck deck clamp
11. Upper deck beam
12. Toptimber
13. Sweep port
14. Sweep port lintel
15. Sweep port sill
16. Lower deck deck clamp
17. Strake above the wale (blackstrake)
18. Main wale and strake between
19. Recess for deck beam end
20. Strake below the deck clamp (beam shelf)
21. Cross chock bolts
22. Strake below the main wale
23. Upper strake of thickstuff over the second futtock heads
24. Diminishing strakes
25. Cross chock, over the first futtock heels
26. Upper strake of the bottom planking
27. Middle band of thickstuff over the first futtock heads
28. Toptimber
29. Joint line of main frame
30. Second futtocks
31. Horizontal bolts between the timbers
32. Lower strake of thickstuff over the floorheads
33. Full or main frame
34. Footwaling
35. Full or main frame
36. Full or main frame
37. Third futtock
38. Keelson
39. Limber strake
40. Keelson scarph
41. First futtocks of a full frame
42. Second futtock
43. First futtock
44. Floor timber
45. Garboard strake
46. Single frames
47. Chock or anchor piece
48. Bed for cross chock
49. First futtock
50. Floor timber
51. Limber hole
52. Reccess for floor timber
53. Bolt holes through floor timber
54. Hog or rising wood
55. Rabbet
56. Keel
57. False keel
A. Scarphs
B. Frame 'B' centre line
C. Frame 'C' centre line
D. Frame 'D' floor

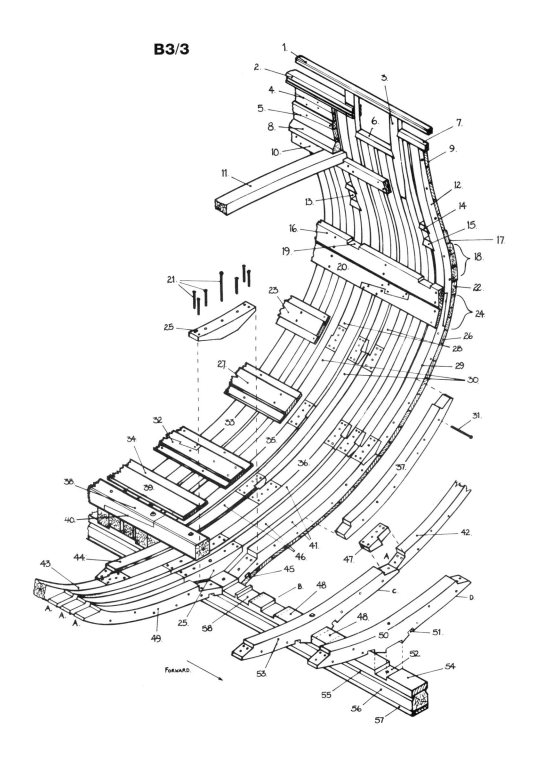

B3/3

FORWARD.

B Hull construction

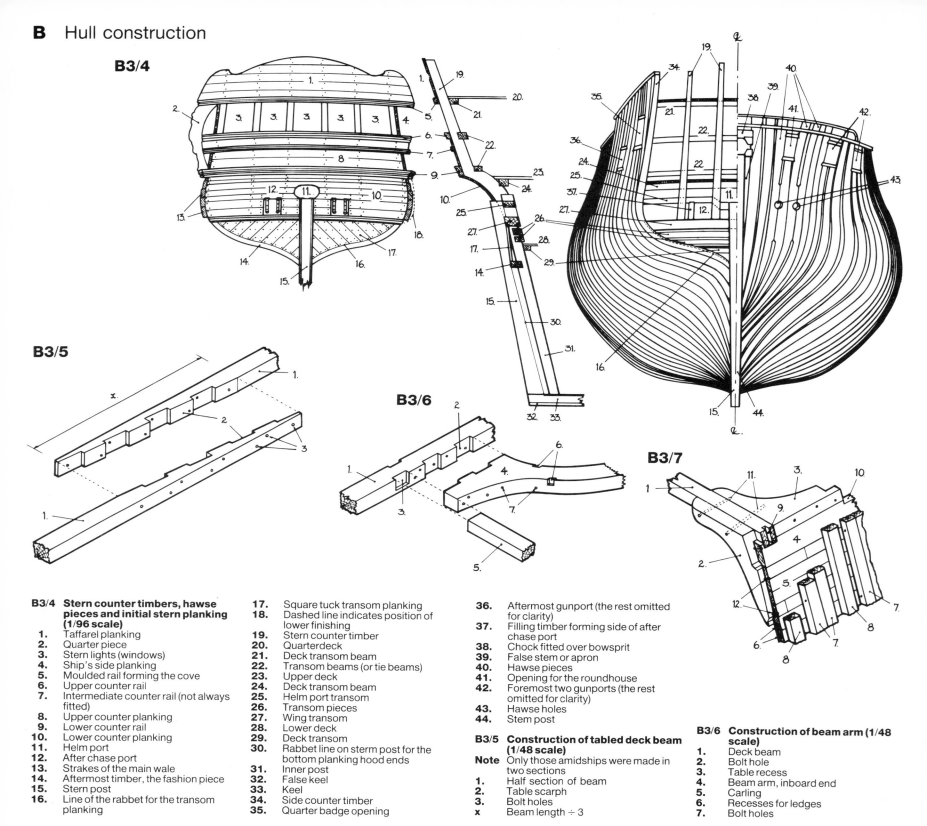

B3/4

B3/5

B3/6

B3/7

B3/4 Stern counter timbers, hawse pieces and initial stern planking (1/96 scale)

1. Taffarel planking
2. Quarter piece
3. Stern lights (windows)
4. Ship's side planking
5. Moulded rail forming the cove
6. Upper counter rail
7. Intermediate counter rail (not always fitted)
8. Upper counter planking
9. Lower counter rail
10. Lower counter planking
11. Helm port
12. After chase port
13. Strakes of the main wale
14. Aftermost timber, the fashion piece
15. Stern post
16. Line of the rabbet for the transom planking

17. Square tuck transom planking
18. Dashed line indicates position of lower finishing
19. Stern counter timber
20. Quarterdeck
21. Deck transom beam
22. Transom beams (or tie beams)
23. Upper deck
24. Deck transom beam
25. Helm port transom
26. Transom pieces
27. Wing transom
28. Lower deck
29. Deck transom
30. Rabbet line on stern post for the bottom planking hood ends
31. Inner post
32. False keel
33. Keel
34. Side counter timber
35. Quarter badge opening

36. Aftermost gunport (the rest omitted for clarity)
37. Filling timber forming side of after chase port
38. Chock fitted over bowsprit
39. False stem or apron
40. Hawse pieces
41. Opening for the roundhouse
42. Foremost two gunports (the rest omitted for clarity)
43. Hawse holes
44. Stem post

B3/5 Construction of tabled deck beam (1/48 scale)

Note Only those amidships were made in two sections

1. Half section of beam
2. Table scarph
3. Bolt holes
x Beam length ÷ 3

B3/6 Construction of beam arm (1/48 scale)

1. Deck beam
2. Bolt hole
3. Table recess
4. Beam arm, inboard end
5. Carling
6. Recesses for ledges
7. Bolt holes

42

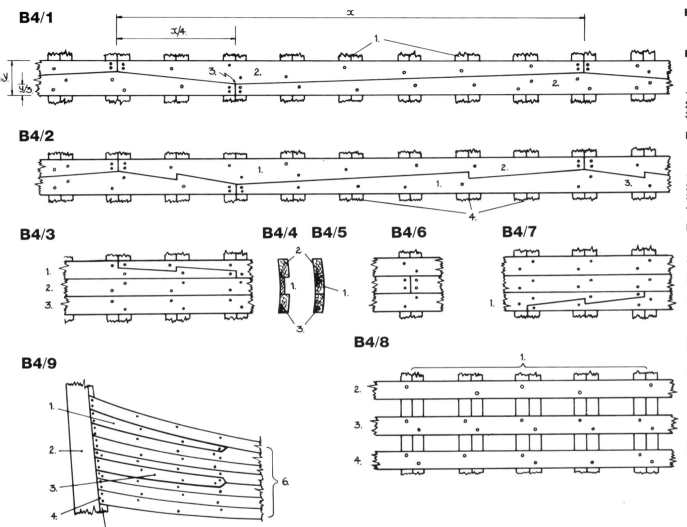

B4/1

B4/2

B4/3   **B4/4** **B4/5**   **B4/6**   **B4/7**

B4/8

B4/9

B4   INTERNAL AND EXTERNAL PLANKING TECHNIQUES (1/48 scale)

B4/1 Top and butt planking (employed for the spirketting and later for the solid built main wale and the various bands of thickstuff)
1. Main timbers (or frames)
2. Single plank, fashioned top and butt
3. The 'touch' of the plank

B4/2 Hook and butt planking (stronger version of the top and butt fashion, usually employed for the solid built main wales)
1. Single plank, fashioned hook and butt
2. Long hook scarph
3. Short hook scarph
4. Timbers (or frames)

B4/3 Detail of the main wale
1. Upper strake of main wale with hook scarph
2. Filling strake (or plank between the wales)
3. Lower strake of the main wale

B4/4 Cross-section of the main wale, c1719
1. Filling strake, half the thickness of the strakes of the main wale
2. Upper strake of the main wale
3. Lower strake of the main wale

B4/5 Cross-section of the main wale (solid built), c1730
1. Filling strake (made up to thickness of the upper and lower strakes. Was often, during a transition period, built up with planking of suitable thickness over original filling strake)
2. Upper strake of the main wale
3. Lower strake of the main wale

B4/6 Butt joint of the filling strake

B4/7 Detail of the lower strake of the main wale
1. Reverse direction hook scarph

B4/8 Methods of securing planking with trennals
Note The butt ends of the planks would have been secured with two nails or dumps
1. Timbers (or frames)
2. Single fastening method
3. Double fastening method
4. Combined single and double method

B4/9 Dropstrakes and stealers (no scale; worked in at the ends of the bottom planking strakes to reduce 'sny' at the hood ends. Either or both were employed as required. They were also used for planking the stem of the ship)
1. Dropstrake
2. Stern post
3. Stealer
4. Hood ends of the planks
5. Rabbet of the stern post
6. Bottom planking

C Internal hull

C1 ARRANGEMENTS

C1/1 Longitudinal section (1/96 scale)

1. Stern counter timber
2. Sheave block
3. Quarter deck
4. Breast rail
5. Mizzen mast
6. Captain's day cabin
7. Badge light (window)
8. Quarter deck clamp
9. Captain's dining quarters
10. Steering wheel
11. Kevel cleat
12. Main jeer capstan
13. Main jeer bitts
14. Elm tree pump brake
15. Main mast
16. Sheave block
17. Main topsail bitts
18. Cleat
19. Cleat
20. Sheave block
21. Upper deck spirketting
22. Cleat
23. Sheave block
24. Galley flue
25. Pissdale
26. Fish davit cleat
27. Fore jeer bitts
28. Fore mast
29. Belfry
30. Sheave block
31. Forecastle decking
32. Knighthead
33. Bowsprit
34. Figure of the head
35. Head rails
36. Hole for the gammoning
37. Stem post
38. Hawse holes
39. Manger
40. Bowsprit step
41. Larboard fore riding bitt
42. After riding bitts
43. Side cast hanging knee
44. Sweep port
45. Upper deck clamp
46. Lower deck spirketting
47. Pillar
48. Chain pump crank handle
49. Main chain pump
50. Lining or quickwork
51. Upper deck beam
52. Main capstan
53. Standard
54. Wardroom bulkhead
55. Officer's cabin
56. Officer's cabin
57. Tiller
58. Transom knee
59. Wing transom
60. Helm port
61. Sternson knee

C1/1

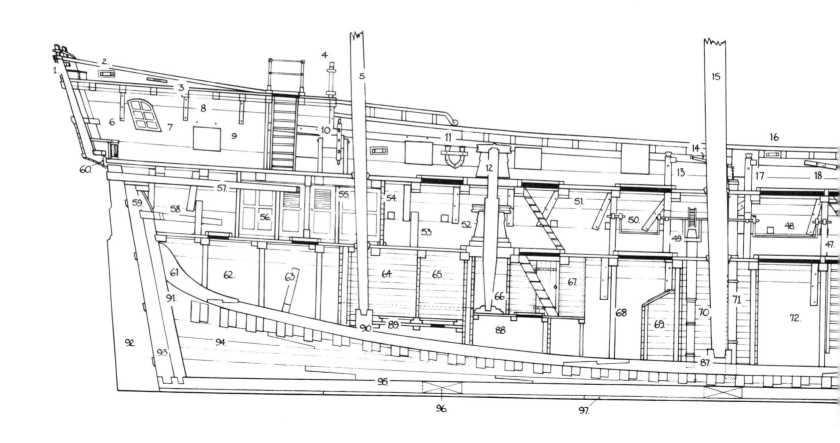

62. Bread room	**78.** Galley stove	**94.** Deadwood
63. Crutch	**79.** Fore peak and sail room	**95.** Keel
64. Filling room	**80.** Stemson	**96.** Scarph of the keel
65. Powder room	**81.** Knee of the head	**97.** False keel
66. Lobby and capstan room	**82.** False stem or apron	**98.** Deadwood or rising wood
67. Captain's store room	**83.** Breast hook	**99.** Gripe and cutwater
68. After hold	**84.** Fore mast step	**100.** Boxing of the stem post
69. Shot locker	**85.** Sail room and coal store	
70. The well	**86.** Keelson	
71. Elm tree pump casing	**87.** Main mast step	
72. Main hold	**88.** Fish room	
73. Hanging knee	**89.** Pallating deck of the magazine	
74. Lower deck clamp	**90.** Mizzen mast step	
75. Pillars	**91.** Inner post	
76. Galley	**92.** Rudder	
77. Galley firehearth	**93.** Stern post	

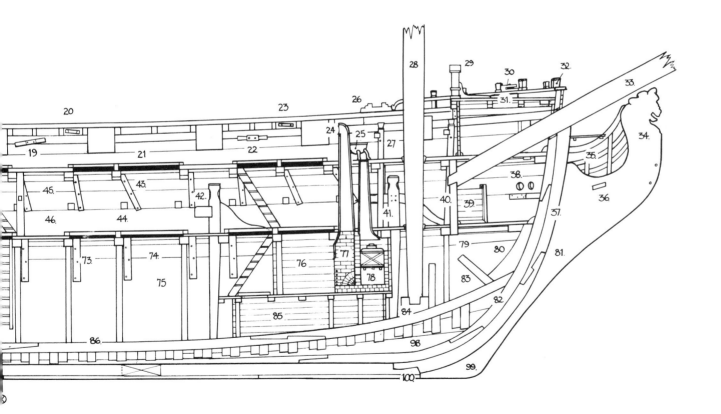

C2/1

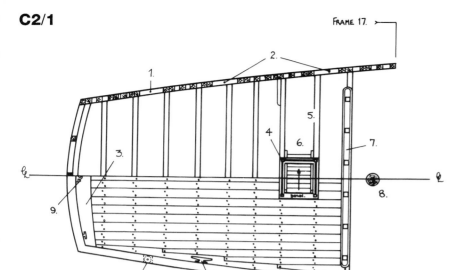

FRAME 17.

C2/2

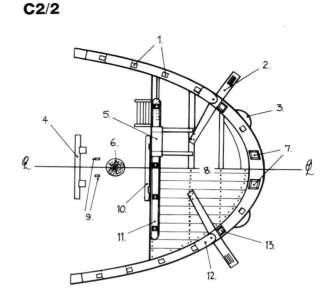

C2

QUARTERDECK AND FORECASTLE

C2/1   Plan view of quarterdeck (1/96 scale)
1. Cabin light
2. Gunports
3. Pendant lockers
4. Companion rail
5. Quarterdeck beam
6. Companionway
7. Quarterdeck breast rail
8. Mizzen mast
9. Tabernacle for ensign staff
10. Sheave
11. Cleat

C2/2   Plan view of forecastle (1/96 scale)
1. Timberheads
2. Cathead
3. Roundhouse
4. Fore jeer bitts
5. Belfry
6. Fore mast
7. Knightheads
8. Forecastle deck
9. Ringbolts for jeers
10. Fore topsail sheet bitts
11. Forecastle breast rail
12. Sheave block for catblock tackle
13. Timberhead

C2/3

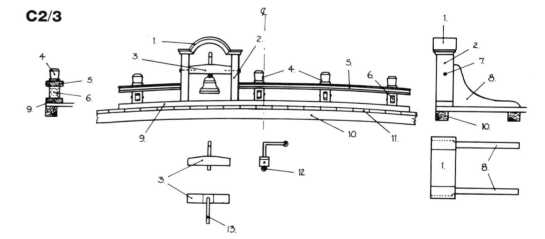

C2/3   The belfry and forecastle breast rail (1/48 scale)
1. Belfry canopy
2. Canopy supports
3. Headstock
4. Breast rail timberheads
5. Rail
6. Sheaves
7. Headstock pivot bolt
8. Standard supporter
9. Rail waterway
10. Forecastle deck beam
11. Deck planking
12. Eye for bell to hang from
13. Attachment for bell cord

C3/1

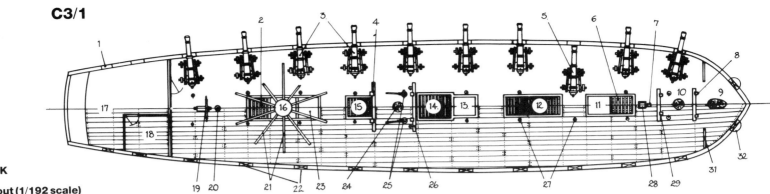

C3   **UPPER DECK**

C3/1   **General layout (1/192 scale)**
1. Quarter light
2. Ventilation grating
3. 6pdr cannon
4. Main jeer bitts
5. Cannon in run in position
6. Ventilation grating
7. Galley ventilation flue
8. Fore topsail sheet bitts
9. Bowsprit
10. Fore mast
11. Fore access hatchway
12. Fore hatch
13. Access hatchway
14. Main hatch
15. After hatch
16. Capstan
17. Captain's day cabin
18. Captain's sleeping berth
19. Steering wheel
20. Mizzen mast
21. Capstan bars (partially omitted for clarity)
22. Gunports
23. After access hatchway
24. Main mast
25. Elm tree pumps
26. Main topsail sheet bitts
27. Ringbolts for the training tackle
28. Galley firehearth flue
29. Fore jeer bitts
30. Forecastle bulkhead
31. Roundhouse

C3/2

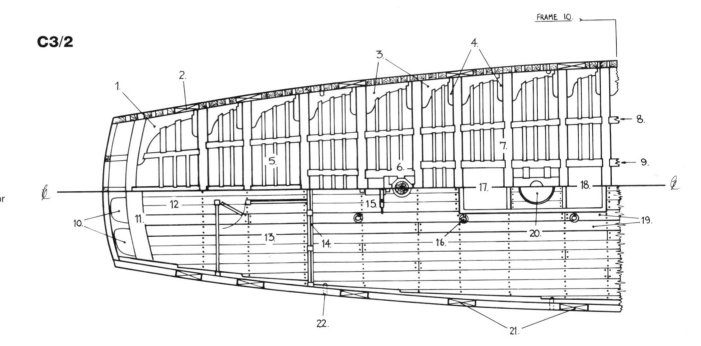

C3/2   **Plan view of after section (1/96 scale)**
1. Transom knee
2. Cabin light
3. Lodging knees
4. Hanging knees
5. Ledges
6. Mizzen mast and partners
7. Upper deck beam
8. Outer tier of carlings
9. Midship tier of carlings
10. Lights (or stern windows)
11. Transom seat
12. Captain's day cabin
13. Captain's sleeping quarters
14. Transverse bulkhead
15. Steering wheel
16. Ringbolt for gun's training tackle
17. Hatchway
18. Access hatchway
19. Binding strakes
20. Capstan
21. Gunports
22. Scupper

C3/3

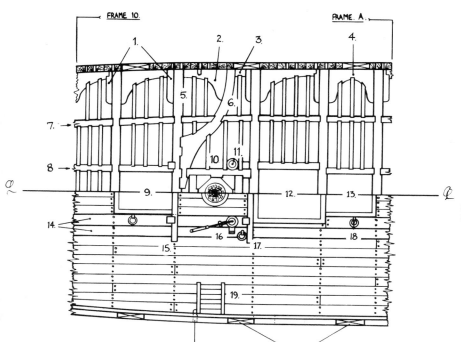

C3/3 Plan view of midship section (1/96 scale)

1. Hanging knees
2. Lodging knee
3. Packing piece
4. Double lodging knee
5. Upper deck beam
6. Beam arm
7. Outer tier of carlings
8. Midship tier of carlings
9. After hatchway
10. Ledges
11. Elm tree pump casing
12. Main hatchway
13. Access hatchway
14. Binding strakes
15. Main jeer bitts
16. Elm tree pump
17. Main topsail sheet bitts
18. Ringbolt for gun's training tackle
19. Gangway to the entry steps
20. Scupper
21. Gunports

C3/4

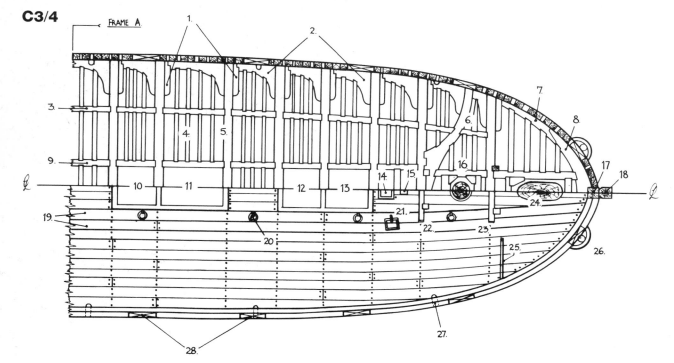

C3/4 Plan view of fore section (1/96 scale)

1. Hanging knees
2. Lodging knees
3. Outer tier of carlings
4. Ledges
5. Upper deck beam
6. Beam arm
7. Ekeing
8. Deck hook
9. Midship tier of carlings
10. Fore hatchway
11. Fore hatchway
12. Access hatchway
13. Ventilation hatchway
14. Galley flue
15. Condensation flue from galley stove
16. Fore mast partners and mast
17. False post or apron
18. Stem post
19. Binding strakes
20. Ringbolt for gun's training tackle
21. Spanshackle
22. Fore jeer bitts
23. Fore topsail sheet bitts
24. Bowsprit
25. Forecastle bulkhead (if fitted)
26. Roundhouse with seat of ease
27. Scupper
28. Gunports

C4/1

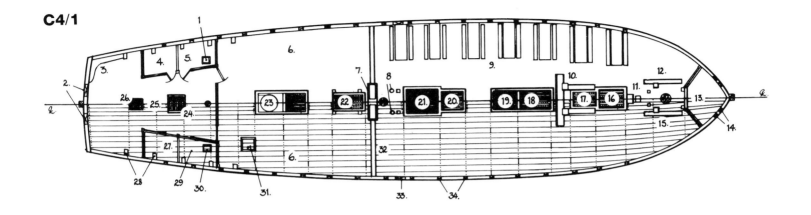

C4 LOWER DECK

C4/1 General layout (1/192 scale)

1. Access scuttle to the bread room
2. After ports
3. Wing transom knee
4. Lieutenant's cabin
5. Surgeon's cabin
6. Area for canvas cabins to be rigged (used by midshipmen/warrant officers etc and probably constituted a separate 'mess')
7. Chain pump cistern
8. Elm tree pump
9. 'Mess' tables and formers
10. After riding bitts
11. Galley flue and vent
12. Port fore riding bitt
13. Manger and bowsprit step
14. Hawse holes
15. Starboard fore riding bitt
16. Ventilation grating
17. Companionway to fore platform
18. Forward hatch
19. Hatchway
20. Companionway to hold
21. Main hatch
22. After hatch
23. Capstan
24. Bread room hatch
25. Wardroom
26. Access scuttle to bread room
27. Master's cabin
28. Standards
29. Cabin
30. Scuttle to magazine lightroom
31. Scuttle to magazine
32. Pump dale
33. Ballast port
34. Sweep ports

C Internal hull

C4/2 Plan view of after section (1/96 scale)

1. Lodging knees
2. Main frames
3. Lower end of the standards
4. Hanging knees
5. Deck transom
6. Scuttle to bread room passageway
7. Outer tier of carlings
8. Stern post
9. Capstan partners
10. After port
11. Ventilation scuttle for the bread room
12. Scuttle to bread room
13. Mizzen mast and partners
14. Wardroom bulkhead
15. Capstan
16. Access hatchway to after platform
17. Midship tier of carlings
18. Officer's cabin
19. Officer's cabin
20. Scuttle to magazine and gunner's store
21. Binding strakes
22. Scuttle to lightroom
23. Waterway
24. Sweep ports
25. Scuttle to magazine and gunner's store
26. Hatch partner (or carling)
27. Hatch ledge
28. Short lodging knee
29. Lower end of the standard

C4/2

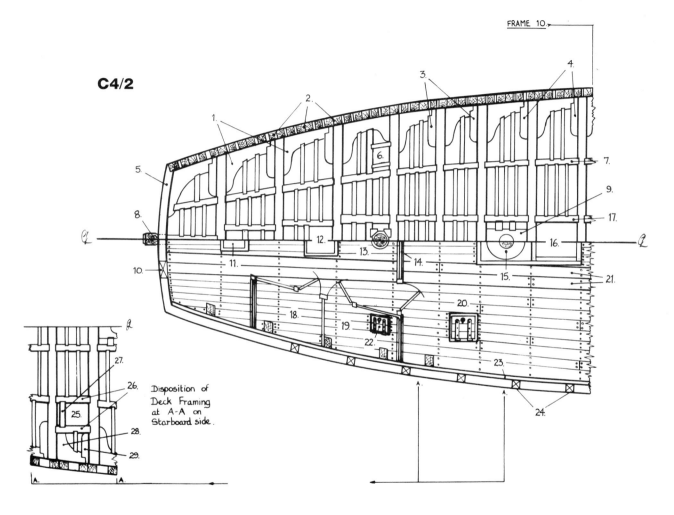

FRAME 10.

Disposition of Deck Framing at A-A on Starboard side.

C4/3 Plan view of midship section (1/96 scale)

1. Lodging knees
2. Filling frame
3. Main frames
4. Hanging knees
5. Double lodging knee
6. Beam arm
7. Outer tier of carlings
8. Ledges
9. Elm tree pump case
10. Lower deck beam
11. Main mast partners
12. After hatchway
13. Main hatchway
14. Access hatchway
15. Midship tier of carlings
16. Chain pump cistern
17. Elm tree pump
18. Binding strakes
19. Chain pump crank handle
20. Chain pump crank handle extension
21. Main hatchway ledge
22. Pump dale
23. Waterway
24. Ballast port
25. Sweep ports

C4/3

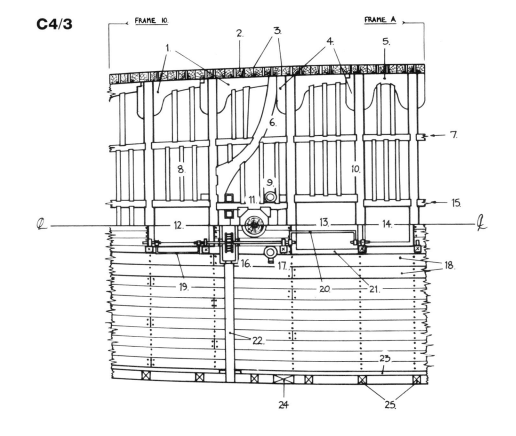

C4/4

FRAME A.

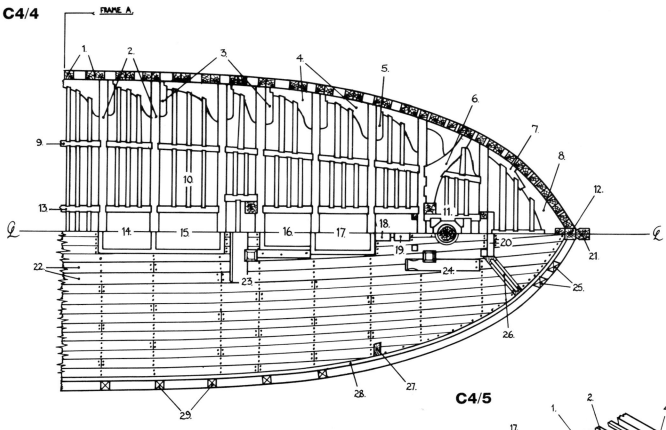

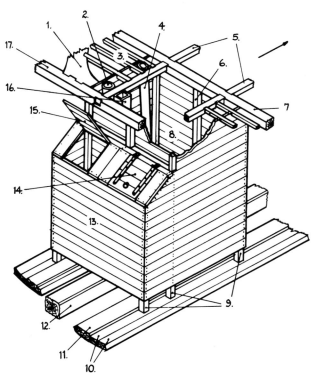

C4/4 Plan view of fore section (1/96 scale)
1. Main frames
2. Lower deck beams
3. Hanging knees
4. Lodging knees
5. Lower end of standard
6. Beam arm
7. Ekeing
8. Deck hook
9. Outer tier of carlings
10. Ledges
11. Fore mast partners
12. False post or apron
13. Midship tier of carlings
14. Fore hatchway
15. Fore hatchway
16. Access hatchway to the fore platform
17. Ventilation hatch for the galley
18. Galley flue
19. Condensation flue from galley stove
20. Manger
21. Stem post
22. Binding strakes
23. After riding bitts
24. Starboard fore riding bitt
25. Hawse holes
26. Manger bulkhead and waterways
27. Standard
28. Waterway
29. Sweep ports

C4/5 Isometric of the pump well (1/64 scale)
1. Beam arm
2. Working chamber of chain pump
3. Ledges
4. Casing of elm tree pump
5. Carlings
6. Centre line stanchion
7. Lower deck beam
8. Pump well
9. Side stanchions
10. Footwaling
11. Limber strake
12. Keelson
13. Shot locker
14. Shot locker scuttle (closed)
15. Shot locker scuttle (open)
16. Lower deck beam

C4/5

C5 PLATFORMS AND HOLD

C5/1 Section of the after platform and hold (no scale)

1. Stern post
2. Inner post
3. Deck transom
4. Lower end of the standards
5. Lodging knee
6. Scuttle ledge
7. Scuttle to bread room passageway
8. External planking
9. Ledges
10. Deck clamp
11. Carling
12. Lobby and capstan room
13. Sternson
14. Pillars
15. Bread room
16. Filling room
17. Powder room
18. Double-lined bulkhead of the magazine
19. Captain's store room and servants' berth
20. Thickstuff over the second futtock heads
21. Lightroom
22. Passageway to magazine
23. Passageway to gunner's store
24. Hatch to fish room
25. Lobby of after platform
26. Thickstuff over the first futtock heads
27. Stern post
28. False keel
29. Keel
30. Spirit room
31. Keelson
32. Thickstuff over the floor heads
33. Limber strake
34. Hog or rising wood

C5/1

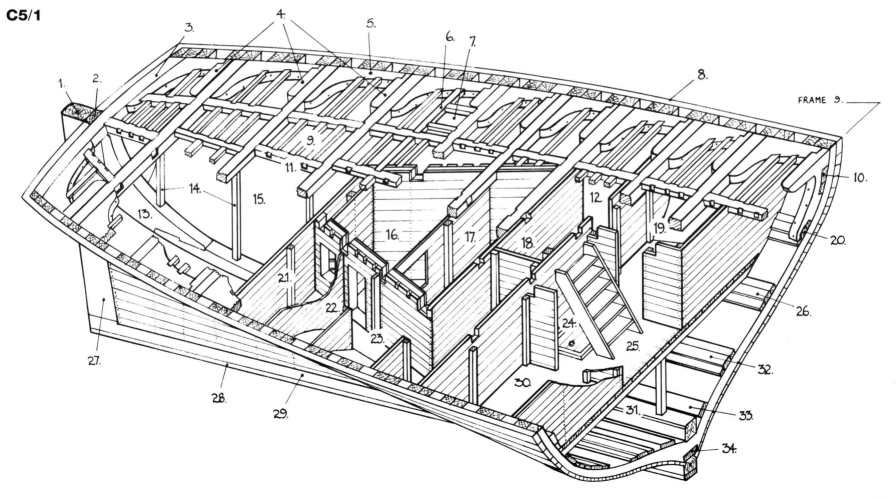

FRAME 9.

C Internal hull

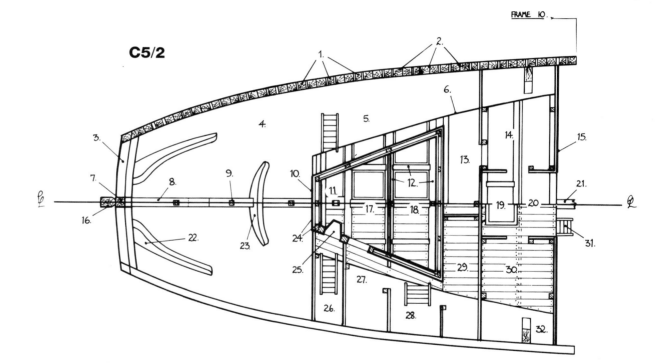

C5/2

C5/3 Section of the fore platform and hold (no scale)

1. Carling (midship tier)
2. Carling (outer tier)
3. Ledges
4. Lower deck beams
5. Lodging knees
6. Lower end of a standard
7. Main frame
8. Cant frame
9. Door to boatswain's store and berth
10. Boatswain's store and berth
11. Beam arm
12. Ekeing
13. Thickstuff over the floor and futtock heads
14. After riding bitt pins
15. Fore mast partners
16. Hawse pieces
17. Deck transom
18. Stemson
19. False stem or apron
20. Galley flue
21. Boatswain's store and sail room
22. Knee of the head
23. Fore and aft bulkhead and coal stowage
24. Fore riding bitt pins
25. Galley firehearth and stove
26. Galley
27. Carpenter's store room
28. After edge of the platform
29. Fore hold (cable tier)
30. Centre line pillar
31. Keelson
32. False keel
33. Keel
34. Boxing
35. Gripe
36. Stem post

C5/3

FRAME 'D'.

55

C Internal hull

C5/4 Plan view of fore platform and forepeak (1/96 scale)
1. Outboard extremity of the fore platform
2. Boatswain's store room and berth
3. Boatswain's store room
4. Breast hook
5. Hawse pieces
6. False stem or apron
7. Bitt pins of the after riding bitts
8. Keelson
9. Hatch to sail room
10. Fore mast step
11. Stem post
12. Hatch to coal store
13. Galley area
14. Galley firehearth
15. Fore part of keelson
16. Stemson
17. Galley stove (kettle)
18. After end of the platform
19. Carpenter's store room and berth
20. Sail room
21. Crutch
22. Bulkhead
23. Deck hook

C5/4

C5/5 Plan view of amidships section of the hold (1/96 scale)
1. Upper band of thickstuff
2. Middle band of thickstuff
3. Ceiling
4. After beam of the fore platform
5. Lower band of thickstuff
6. Back case of the chain pump
7. Casing of the elm tree pump
8. Fore bulkhead of the well
9. Ladder
10. Pillars
11. Main hold
12. After platform
13. Shot locker
14. Pump well
15. Keelson
16. Bitt pins of the after riding bitts
17. Limber strake
18. Ladder to after platform
19. Working chamber of the chain pump
20. Main mast step
21. Casing of the elm tree pump
22. Strake next to the limberstrake (footwaling)
23. Fore platform
24. Shot locker access hatch
25. Spirit room bulkhead
26. Hanging knees
27. Limber channels

C5/5

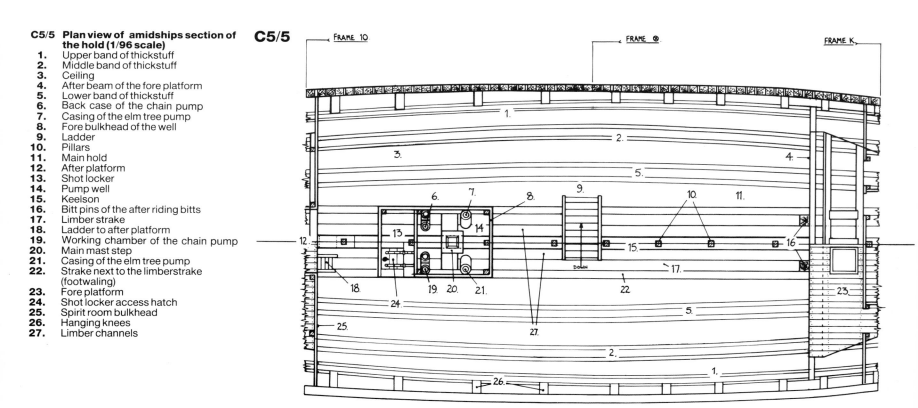

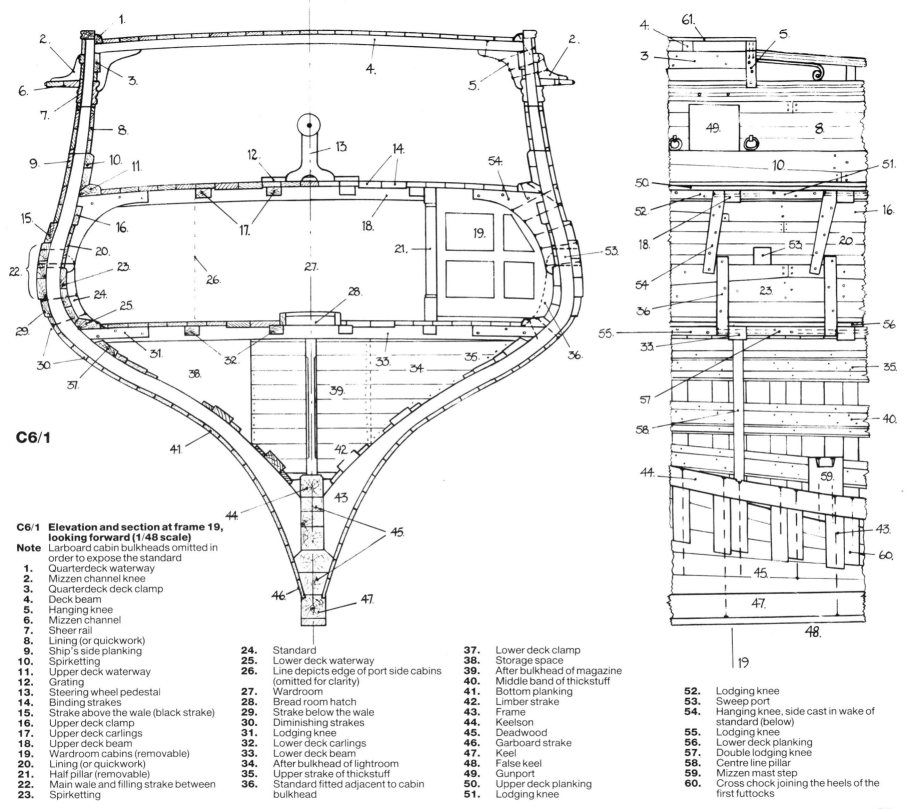

C6/1

C6/1 Elevation and section at frame 19, looking forward (1/48 scale)

Note Larboard cabin bulkheads omitted in order to expose the standard

1. Quarterdeck waterway
2. Mizzen channel knee
3. Quarterdeck deck clamp
4. Deck beam
5. Hanging knee
6. Mizzen channel
7. Sheer rail
8. Lining (or quickwork)
9. Ship's side planking
10. Spirketting
11. Upper deck waterway
12. Grating
13. Steering wheel pedestal
14. Binding strakes
15. Strake above the wale (black strake)
16. Upper deck clamp
17. Upper deck carlings
18. Upper deck beam
19. Wardroom cabins (removable)
20. Lining (or quickwork)
21. Half pillar (removable)
22. Main wale and filling strake between
23. Spirketting

24. Standard
25. Lower deck waterway
26. Line depicts edge of port side cabins (omitted for clarity)
27. Wardroom
28. Bread room hatch
29. Strake below the wale
30. Diminishing strakes
31. Lodging knee
32. Lower deck carlings
33. Lower deck beam
34. After bulkhead of lightroom
35. Upper strake of thickstuff
36. Standard fitted adjacent to cabin bulkhead

37. Lower deck clamp
38. Storage space
39. After bulkhead of magazine
40. Middle band of thickstuff
41. Bottom planking
42. Limber strake
43. Frame
44. Keelson
45. Deadwood
46. Garboard strake
47. Keel
48. False keel
49. Gunport
50. Upper deck planking
51. Lodging knee

52. Lodging knee
53. Sweep port
54. Hanging knee, side cast in wake of standard (below)
55. Lodging knee
56. Lower deck planking
57. Double lodging knee
58. Centre line pillar
59. Mizzen mast step
60. Cross chock joining the heels of the first futtocks

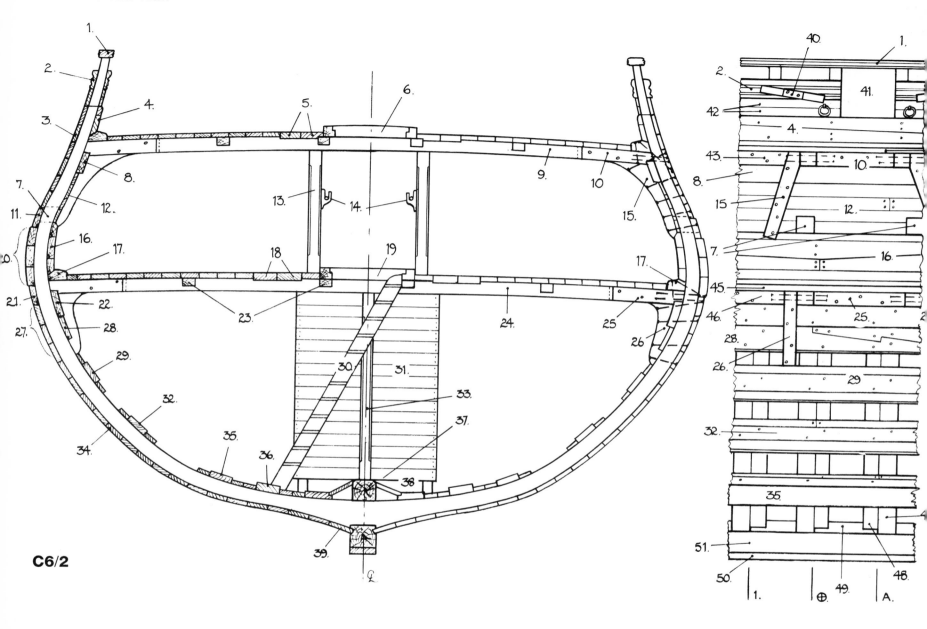

C6/2

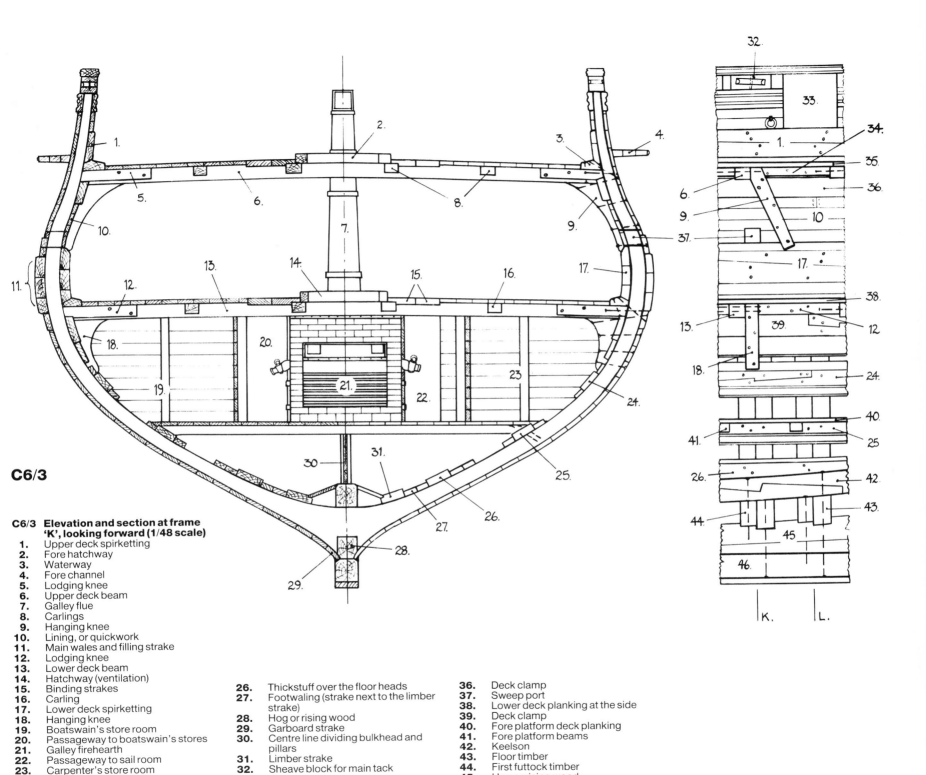

C6/3

C6/3 Elevation and section at frame 'K', looking forward (1/48 scale)

1. Upper deck spirketting
2. Fore hatchway
3. Waterway
4. Fore channel
5. Lodging knee
6. Upper deck beam
7. Galley flue
8. Carlings
9. Hanging knee
10. Lining, or quickwork
11. Main wales and filling strake
12. Lodging knee
13. Lower deck beam
14. Hatchway (ventilation)
15. Binding strakes
16. Carling
17. Lower deck spirketting
18. Hanging knee
19. Boatswain's store room
20. Passageway to boatswain's stores
21. Galley firehearth
22. Passageway to sail room
23. Carpenter's store room
24. Thickstuff over the second futtock heads
25. Thickstuff over the first futtock heads

26. Thickstuff over the floor heads
27. Footwaling (strake next to the limber strake)
28. Hog or rising wood
29. Garboard strake
30. Centre line dividing bulkhead and pillars
31. Limber strake
32. Sheave block for main tack
33. Gunport
34. Lodging knee
35. Upper deck planking at the side

36. Deck clamp
37. Sweep port
38. Lower deck planking at the side
39. Deck clamp
40. Fore platform deck planking
41. Fore platform beams
42. Keelson
43. Floor timber
44. First futtock timber
45. Hog or rising wood
46. Keel

C Internal hull

C7/1
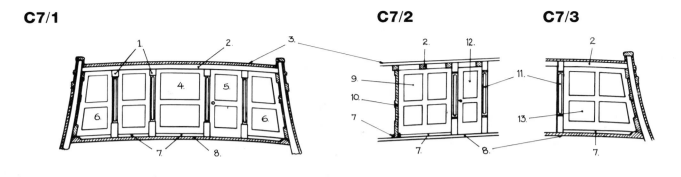

C7/2

C7/3

C7/4
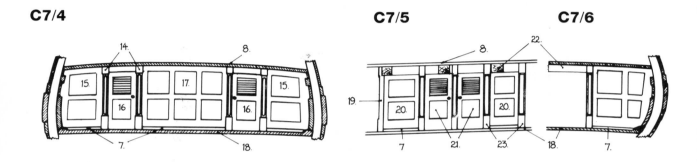

C7/5

C7/6

C7/7

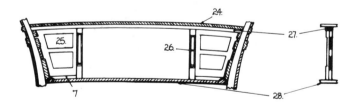

C7 **BULKHEADS OF THE MAIN AND LOWER DECKS (1/96 scale)**

C7/1 Bulkhead below the quarterdeck

C7/2 Captain's bedplace from larboard

C7/3 After side of bedplace

C7/4 Wardroom bulkhead on lower deck

C7/5 Starboard side of wardroom cabins (canvas screens were often used as an alternative to the wardroom cabin and captain's bedplace timber bulkheads)

C7/6 After side of wardroom cabins

C7/7 Half bulkheads below the forecastle (not always fitted)

1. Pillars
2. Quarterdeck beam
3. Quarterdeck planking
4. Centre panel (portable)
5. Door to captain's quarters
6. Side panel (portable)
7. Combined waterway and locating beam
8. Upper deck planking
9. Panel (portable)
10. Pillar
11. Pillar
12. Door to captain's bedplace
13. Panel (portable)
14. Pillars
15. Side panel (portable)
16. Doors to the wardroom
17. Centre panel (portable)
18. Lower deck planking
19. Pillar
20. Panels (portable)
21. Cabin doors
22. Upper deck beams
23. Pillars
24. Forecastle deck planking
25. Side panels (not always fitted)
26. Pillar (not always fitted)
27. Forecastle beam
28. Upper deck planking

C8/1

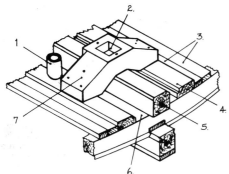

C8/2

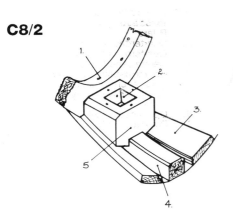

C8/4

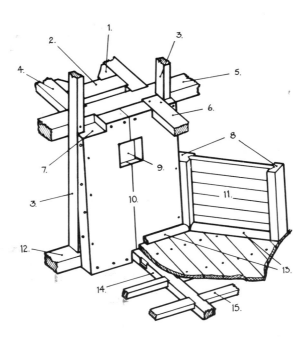

C8/3

C Internal hull

C9   BITTS (1/48 scale)

C9/1   Starboard side elevation of aftermost riding bitt

C9/2   Section elevation viewed from aft of starboard aftermost riding bitt
1. Bitt pins
2. Cross piece
3. Standard
4. Carling of greater scantling
5. Tabling of standard into carling
6. Lower deck beam
7. Platform beam
8. Keelson
9. Limber strake and footwaling
10. Binding strakes

C9/3   Starboard side elevation of foremost riding bitt

C9/4   Section elevation of starboard foremost riding bitt
1. Bitt pins
2. Combined support and securing timber
3. Lower deck beam
4. Fore bulkhead of galley
5. Platform beam
6. Rising of the keelson
7. Limber strake and footwaling

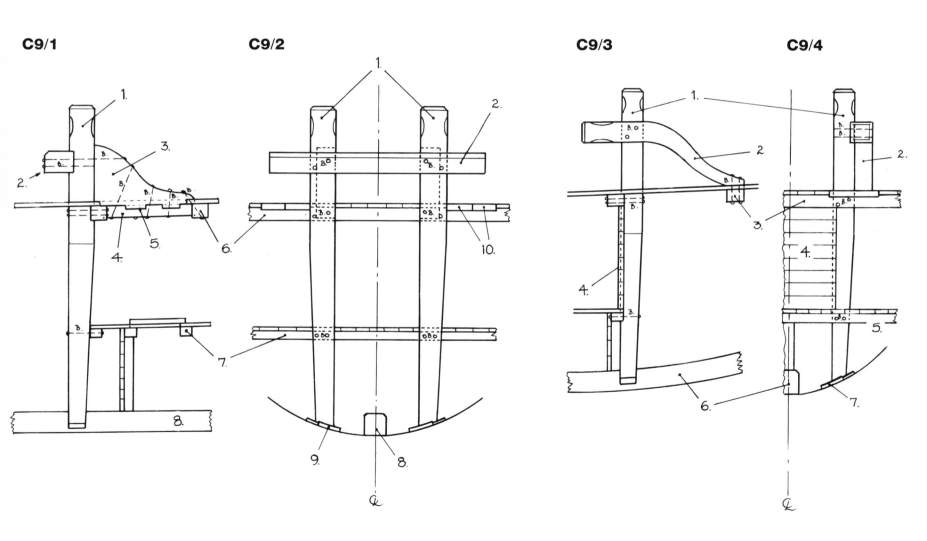

C9/1   C9/2   C9/3   C9/4

C9/5

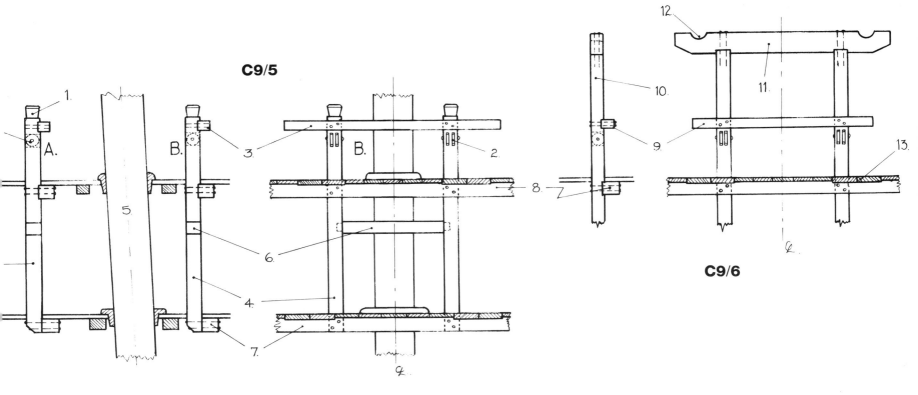

C9/7

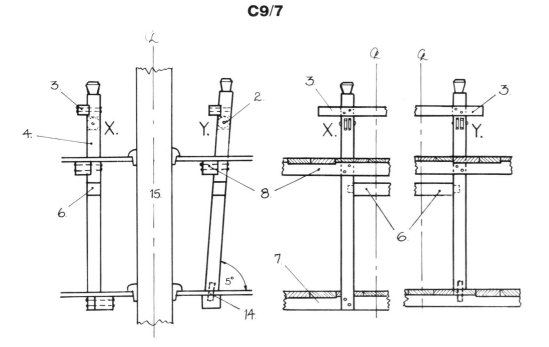

C9/6

D External hull

D1 GENERAL

D1/1 Starboard side, based on Science Museum model (no scale)

D1/1

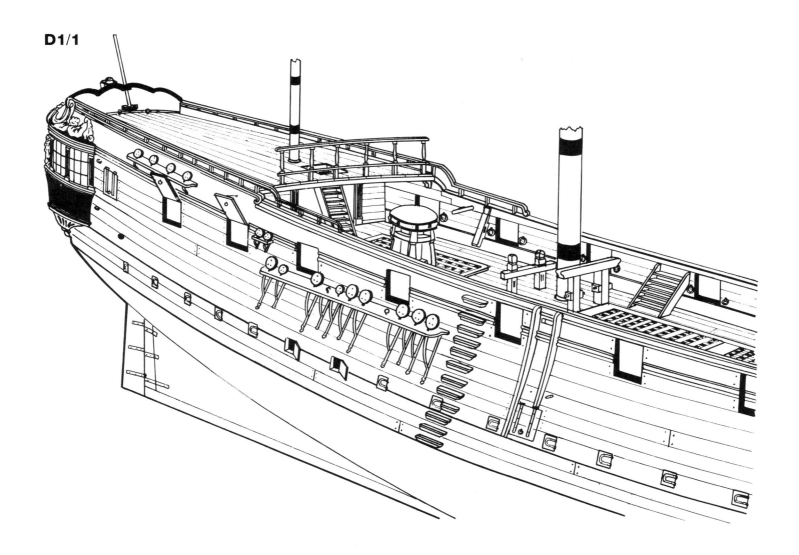

D1/2

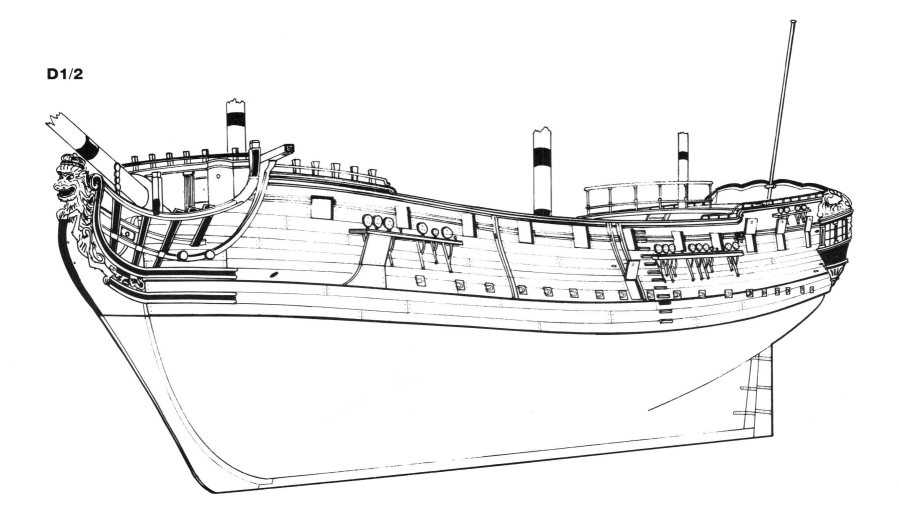

D Externalhull

D1/3 Disposition of the external features and planking strakes (1/192 scale)

1. Taffarel
2. Quarter badge
3. Mizzen topmast backstay deadeye
4. Fife rail
5. Mizzen channel
6. Eyebolt for the main sheet
7. Sheave block for the main sheet
8. Main topmast backstay stool
9. Main channel
10. Entry ladder steps
11. Sheave block for the fore sheet
12. Fenders
13. Eyebolt for the fore sheet
14. Planksheer
15. Sheave block for the spritsail sheet
16. Sheer rail
17. Chesstree
18. Fore topmast backstay stool
19. Sheave block for the main tack
20. Fore channel
21. Fish davit cleat
22. Eyebolt for the spritsail sheet
23. Eyebolt for the bowsprit shroud

24. Fife rail
25. Cathead
26. Roundhouse
27. Head rails
28. Counter rail
29. Square tuck transom
30. Rudder
31. Gudgeon braces
32. Eyebolt for the main brace
33. Strake above the wales (black strake)
34. Sweep ports
35. Keel
36. False keel
37. Scupper discharges
38. Chain pump discharge scupper
39. Ballast port
40. Rabbet of the keel
41. Hook and butt scarphing
42. Upper and lower strakes of the main wale
43. Filling strake between the wales
44. Anchor lining
45. Manger scuppers
46. Hawse holes
47. Trailboard
48. Slot for the gammon lashing

D1/3

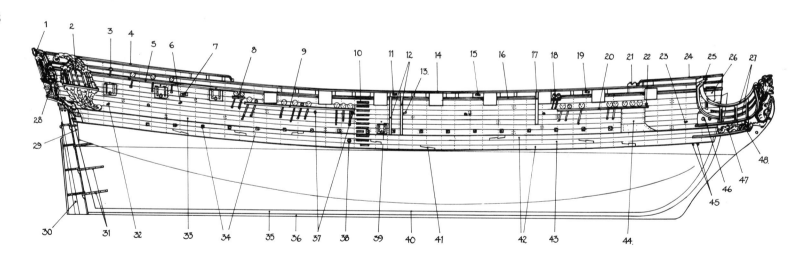

D2/1

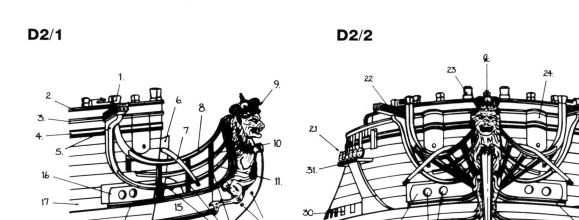

D2/2

D2/3

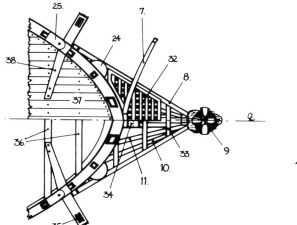

D2/4

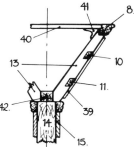

D2	**HEAD OF THE SHIP (1/96 scale)**
D2/1	**Side view**
D2/2	**Front view**
D2/3	**Plan**
D2/4	**Cross section (twice scale)**

1.	Timberhead
2.	Fife rail
3.	Drift rail
4.	Sheer rail
5.	Cathead supporter knee
6.	Head of the stem post
7.	Boomkin
8.	Main head rail
9.	Figurehead
10.	Middle head rail
11.	Lower head rail
12.	Holes for the bobstays
13.	Head timbers
14.	Knee of the head
15.	Trailboard
16.	Hawse lining
17.	Strake above the wales (black strake)
18.	Upper and lower strakes of the main wale
19.	Hair bracket
20.	Lower cheek bracket
21.	Fore mast deadeyes
22.	Cathead
23.	Knighthead timber
24.	Roundhouse
25.	Catblock sheave block
26.	Gunports
27.	Anchor lining
28.	Strake between the wales
29.	Hawse holes
30.	Sweep ports
31.	Fore channel
32.	Grating (forming beakhead)
33.	Beakhead support beam
34.	Hole for the main stay collar
35.	Sheave slot for catblock tackle
36.	Forecastle beams
37.	Forecastle deck
38.	Cattail
39.	Head timber moulding
40.	Beakhead support beam
41.	Knee
42.	Lacing

D External hull

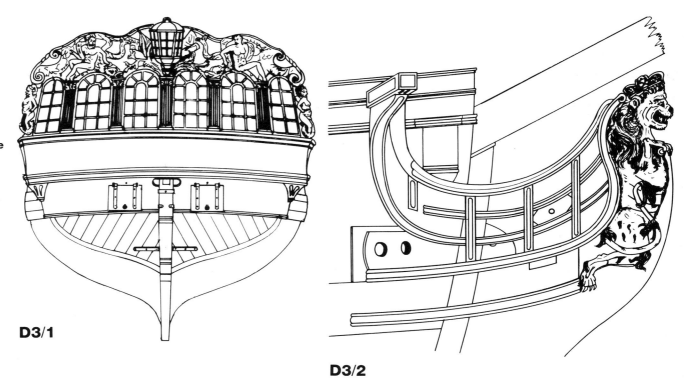

D3/1

D3/2

D3/3

D3/4

D3/5

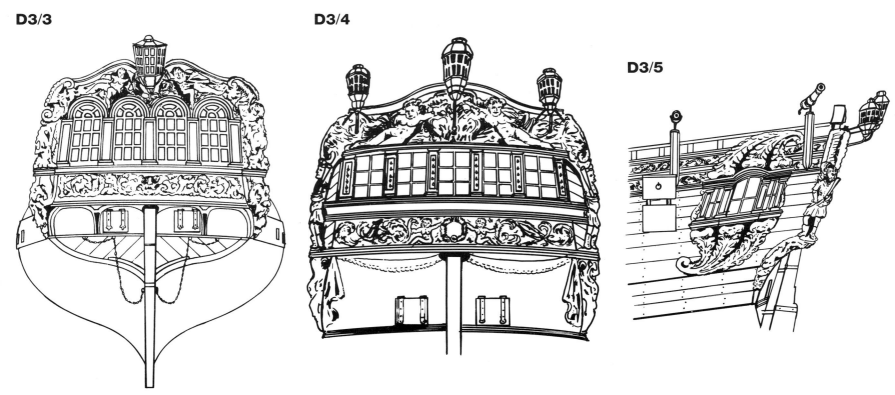

D4 **STYLES OF QUARTER GALLERY**
(1/96 scale)

D4/1 *Bideford* of 1727

D4/2 *Dolphin* of 1731

D4/3 Quarter and stern of *Garland*,
after great repair completed
August 1736

D4/1

D4/2

D4/3

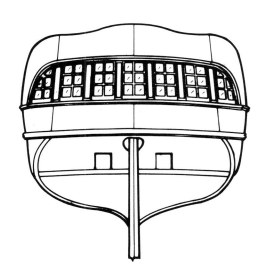

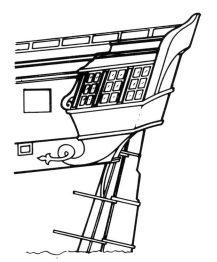

D External hull

D5 **DETAIL OF ENTRY STEPS AND**
   FENDERS (1/645 scale)

D5/1 **Side view**

D5/2 **Section A–A**

D5/3 **Section B–B**
   1. Entry steps or ladder
   2. Sheave for the fore sheet
   3. Planksheer
   4. Gunport
   5. Main channel board
   6. Fenders
   7. Black strake
   8. Ballast port
   9. Filling strake
   10. Main wales
   11. Pump dale scupper
   12. Sweep ports

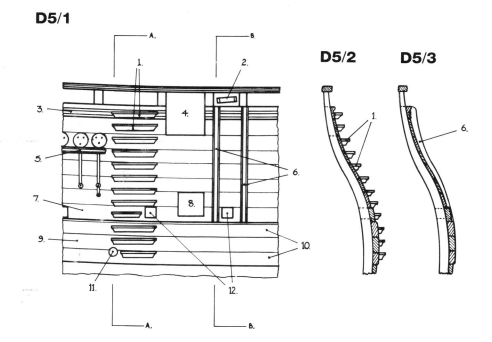

D5/1

D5/2   **D5/3**

E Fittings

E1 THE RUDDER, TILLER AND STEERING WHEEL

E1/1 Side and rear view of rudder (1/48 scale)

E1/2 Elevation of tiller (1/48 scale)

E1/3 Plan view of steering mechanism (1/48 scale)

1. Mortice to receive the tiller
2. Iron binding straps
3. Bearding
4. Ringbolt for rudder chains
5. Brace
6. Pintle
7. Stern post
8. The back piece
9. Bolt
10. Main piece
11. Gudgeon
12. Keel
13. Sole
14. False keel
15. Upper deck beams
16. Gooseneck
17. Cleat for the tiller ropes
18. Iron hoop and eyes
19. Tiller
20. Tiller quadrant
21. Helm port
22. Rudder head or stock
23. Tiller ropes
24. Tiller block
25. Eyebolt

E1/1

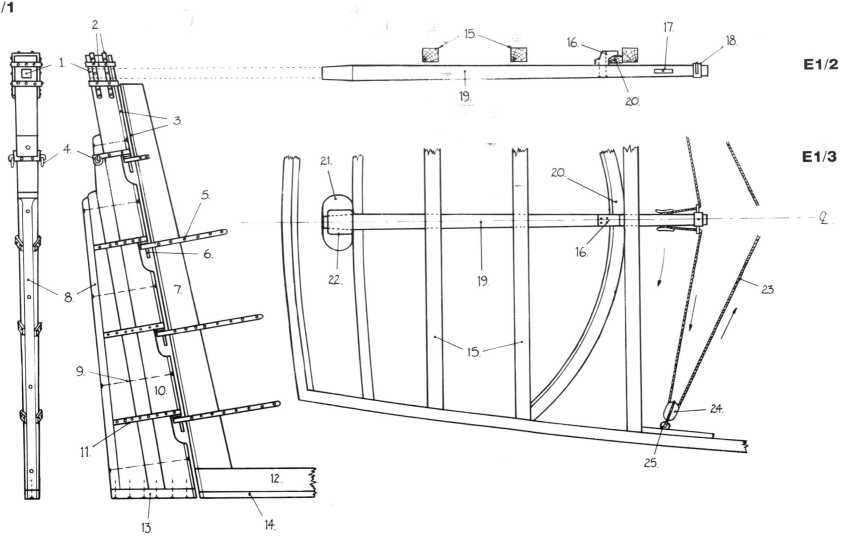

E1/2

E1/3

E Fittings

E1/4

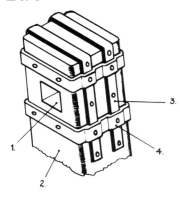

E1/5

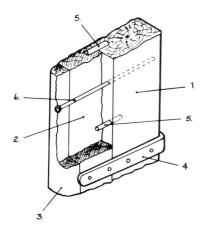

E1/6

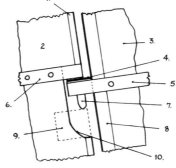

E1/7

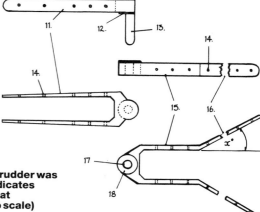

E1/6   Side view of how the rudder was hung (dashed line indicates rudder lock inserted at uppermost brace. No scale)

E1/7   Details of gudgeons and pintles (1/24 scale)
1. Bearding of the rudder
2. Main piece
3. Stern post
4. Copper washer
5. Gudgeon brace
6. Pintle brace
7. Gudgeon pin (pintle)
8. Bearding of the stern post
9. Position of rudder lock if fitted
10. Recess for clearance
11. Pintle brace
12. Land for the washer
13. Gudgeon pin (pintle)
14. Bolt hole
15. Gudgeon brace
16. Space for variation of brace length
17. Hole for pintle
18. Land for washer

E1/8   Side view of single type steering wheel (1/48 scale)

E1/9   Front view of single type steering wheel (1/48 scale)
1. Drum
2. Tiller transmission rope
3. Steering wheel
4. Fore support stanchion
5. After support stanchion
6. Wooden spacing block or foot
7. Brass stiffening plate
8. Slots for transmission rope

E1/4   Detail of the rudder head (no scale)
1. Mortice for the tiller
2. Rudder head
3. Vertical iron strapping
4. Iron hoops

E1/5   The construction of the rudder (no scale)
1. The main piece
2. Extension piece
3. Back piece
4. Pintle brace
5. Coak (dowel)
6. Bolt

E1/8

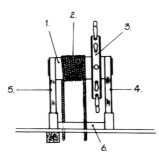

E1/9

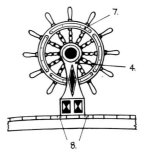

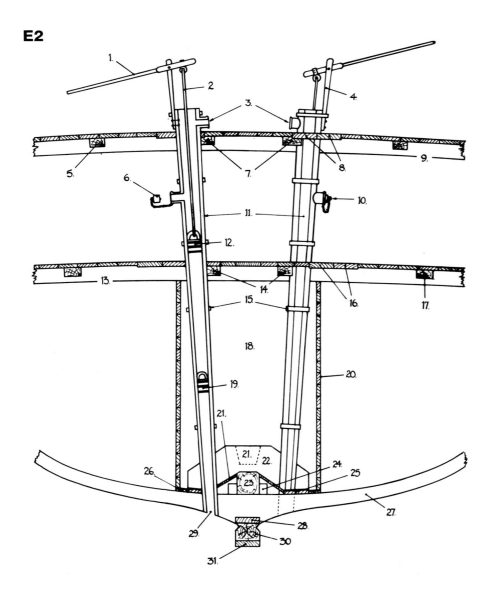

E2

E3/1

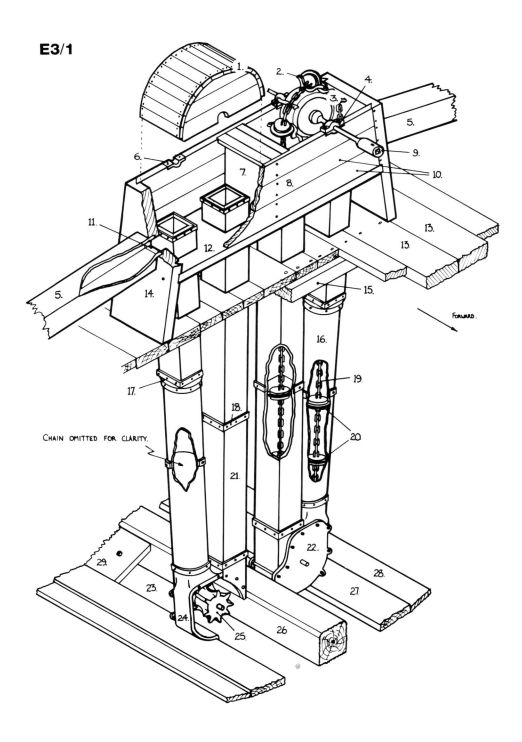

CHAIN OMITTED FOR CLARITY.

FORWARD.

E3/4

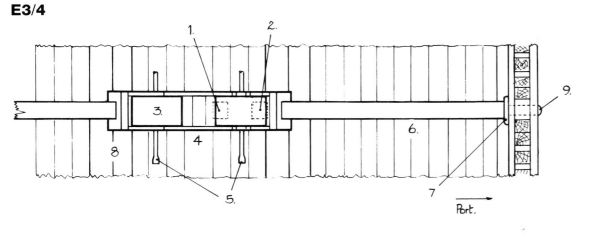

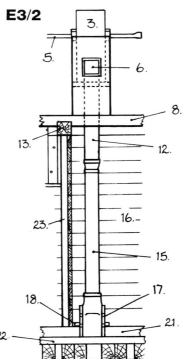

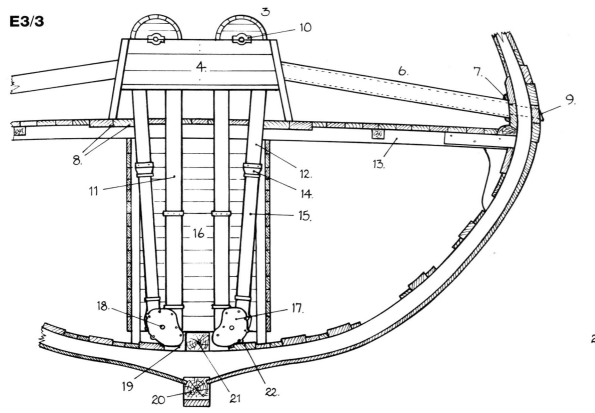

E3/3

E3/2

Port.

E3/2 **Starboard side view (1/48 scale)**

E3/3 **Athwartship view (1/48 scale)**

E3/4 **Plan (1/48 scale)**
1. Back case
2. Return case (or working chamber)
3. Sprocket wheel cover
4. Cistern
5. Crank shafts
6. Pump dale
7. Retaining block
8. Binding strakes
9. Lead scupper
10. Shaft bearing
11. Back case
12. Return case
13. Lower deck beam
14. Transition piece between square and round section of the working chamber
15. Working chamber
16. Pump well
17. Lower sprocket wheel cover plate
18. Sprocket wheel spindle
19. Limber passage
20. Keel
21. Keelson
22. Limber strake
23. Centre line pillar

75

E Fittings

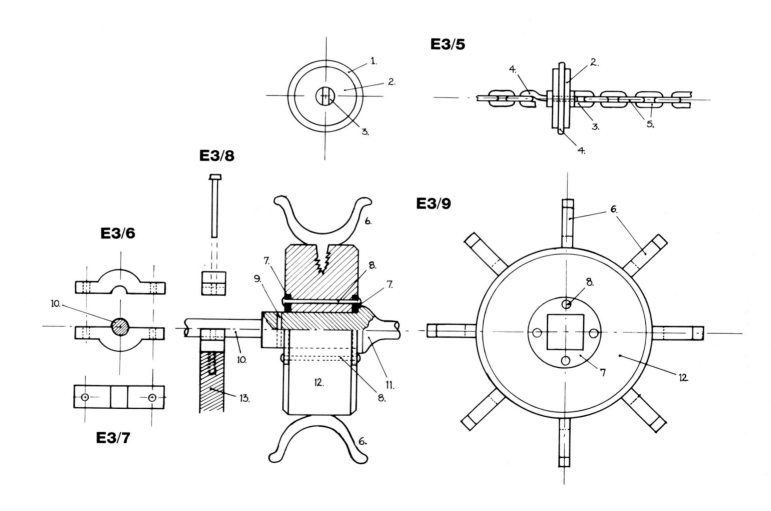

E3/5

E3/8

E3/6

E3/7

E3/9

E3/10 Spindle (1/8 scale)

E3/11 Crank handle (1/8 scale)

E3/12 Spindle connection socket (1/8 scale)

E3/13 Spindle stop (1/8 scale)

E3/14 Cotter (1/8 scale)

E3/10

E3/11

E3/12

E3/13

E3/14

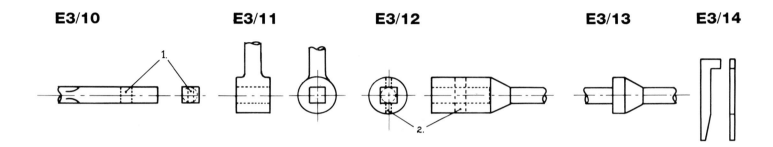

E3/15 Fore and aft view of brackets supporting crank handles (1/8 scale)

E3/16 Inboard face of brackets supporting crank handles (1/8 scale)

1. Slot for cotter pin
2. Slot for cotter pin
3. Pillar
4. Support bracket
5. Bolt holes
6. Retaining pin hole
7. Crank handle shaft
8. Fore lock cotter or gib
9. Washer
10. Fore lock bolt
11. Retaining pin

E3/15

E3/16

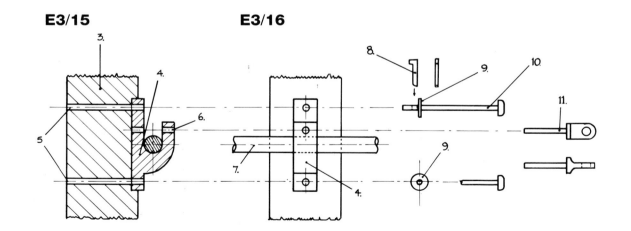

E Fittings

E4 **MAIN JEER CAPSTAN AS FITTED TO A 20-GUN SHIP OF *c*1720 (1/48 scale)**

E4/1 **Side view of the capstan**

E4/2 **Section of the drumhead**

E4/3 **Capstan bars**

E4/4 **Plan through X — X**

E4/5 **Alternative form of lower spindle**
1. Sockets for the capstan bars
2. Drumhead
3. Upper chock piece
4. Whelp
5. Lower chock piece
6. Capstan partners
7. Upper deck beam
8. Barrel (often referred to as the spindle)
9. Upper chock piece
10. Whelps
11. Lower chock piece
12. Iron spindle
13. Iron pawls
14. Capstan step
15. Iron saucer for the spindle
16. Lower deck beams
17. Bolt hole
18. Square mortice for the batten head tenon
19. Plan view of the bar
20. Side elevation of the bar
21. Slot for the swifter rope
22. Head ledges
23. Lower portion of the barrel spindle
24. Iron plate or saucer
25. Capstan step
26. After platform deck

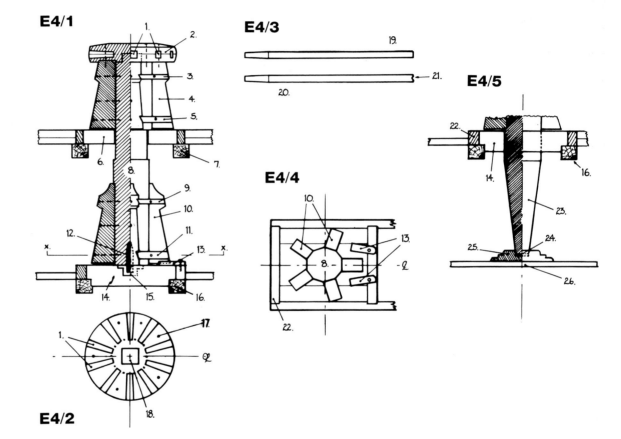

E5 ANCHORS

E5/1 Sheet or bower anchor (drawn from dimensions given in Sutherland's *Shipbuilding Unveiled*, 1717. Weight 18cwt 1qtr. 1/48 scale)

1. Iron bands
2. Anchor ring
3. Hole for the anchor ring
4. Nut (or shoulder)
5. Square of the shank
6. Anchor stock (oak)
7. Two halves of the stock
8. Small of the shank
9. Shank
10. Trend (balance point)
11. Chamfered edging
12. Palm
13. Arm
14. Throat
15. Snipe
16. Blade
17. Bill
18. Crown

E5/2 Kedge anchor, *c*1720 (1/48 scale)

E5/1

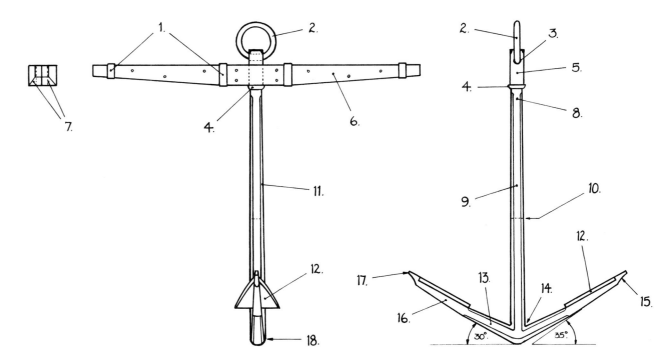

E5/2

E Fittings

E5/3

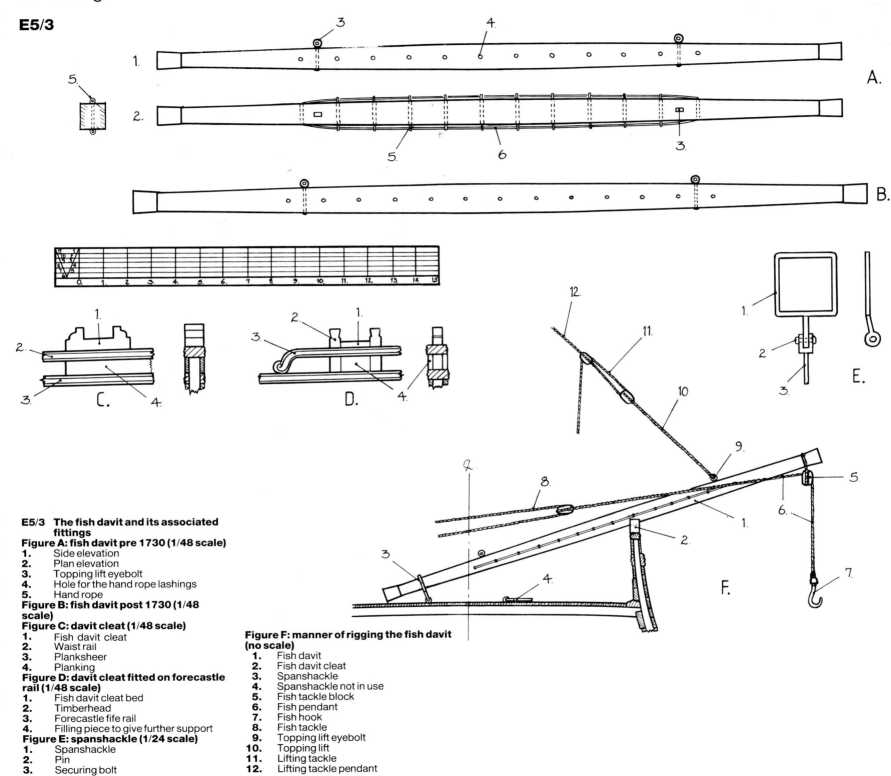

E5/3   The fish davit and its associated fittings

Figure A: fish davit pre 1730 (1/48 scale)
1. Side elevation
2. Plan elevation
3. Topping lift eyebolt
4. Hole for the hand rope lashings
5. Hand rope

Figure B: fish davit post 1730 (1/48 scale)

Figure C: davit cleat (1/48 scale)
1. Fish davit cleat
2. Waist rail
3. Plank sheer
4. Planking

Figure D: davit cleat fitted on forecastle rail (1/48 scale)
1. Fish davit cleat bed
2. Timberhead
3. Forecastle fife rail
4. Filling piece to give further support

Figure E: spanshackle (1/24 scale)
1. Spanshackle
2. Pin
3. Securing bolt

Figure F: manner of rigging the fish davit (no scale)
1. Fish davit
2. Fish davit cleat
3. Spanshackle
4. Spanshackle not in use
5. Fish tackle block
6. Fish pendant
7. Fish hook
8. Fish tackle
9. Topping lift eyebolt
10. Topping lift
11. Lifting tackle
12. Lifting tackle pendant

E5/4 Manner in which the anchors were stowed (1/96 scale)

E5/4

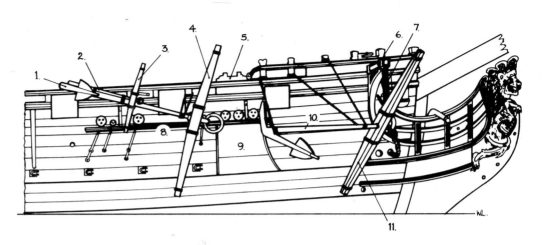

E5/5 Puddening of the anchor ring (no scale)

E5/6 Anchor buoy rope (no scale)

E5/7 Anchor buoy (no scale)
- **1.** Sheet anchor
- **2.** Kedge anchor
- **3.** Kedge anchor stock
- **4.** Sheet anchor stock
- **5.** Fish davit cleat
- **6.** Cathead
- **7.** Cat block tackle
- **8.** Fore channel
- **9.** Anchor lining and billboard
- **10.** Bower anchor
- **11.** Bower anchor stock

E5/5

E5/7

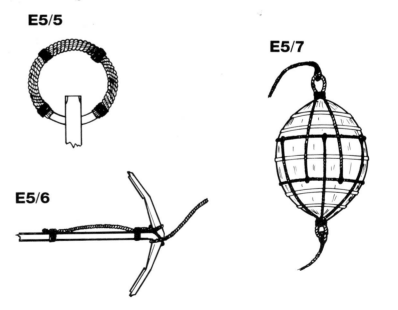

E5/6

E Fittings

E5/8 Side view of the anchor lining (1/48 scale)

E5/9 Section A—A of anchor lining (1/48 scale)

1. 'Finger & thumb' timberheads
2. Fish davit cleat
3. Fife rail
4. Planksheer
5. Gunport
6. Knee
7. Fore channel board
8. Billboard
9. Bolster
10. Sweep port
11. Black strake
12. Main wales
13. Filling strake
14. Chains

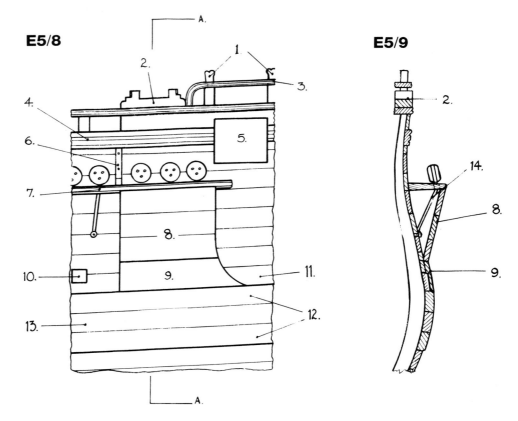

E5/8

E5/9

E6 **THE GALLEY FIREHEARTH, COPPER KETTLES AND OVENS**
(1/48 scale)
Kettle capacity 15.5 gallons.
Oven capacity 8 square feet, each
oven being divided into 2 tiers,
each 4 square feet.

E6/1 Detail of top portion of galley flue

E6/2 Side elevation of firehearth

E6/3 Front elevation of firehearth

E6/4 Sectional elevation

E6/5 Section A—A

E6/6 Section B—B

E6/7 Plan section X—X (top) and at Y—Y (bottom)

E6/8 Plan of starboard kettle (twice scale)

E6/9 Detail of copper kettle
1. Iron strapping
2. Drain cock
3. Kettle lid
4. Oven door
5. Iron support bracket
6. Grate bars
7. Baffle
8. Smoke flue
9. Condensation flue
10. Copper kettle
11. Heat ducts to oven
12. Oven space
13. Heat ducts to kettles
14. Heat outlet ducts to flue
15. Baffle
16. Cross section of firehearth brickwork
17. Iron plate supporting hearth floor
18. Nozzle and drain cock
19. Oven grill bars
20. Air space to reduce heat transfer to decking
21. Centre supporting brickwork
22. Firehearth
23. Kettle enclosure brickwork
24. Kettle lid
25. Kettle support bricks
26. Heat space below kettle
27. Spit support and bracket
28. Kettle drain cock
29. Pipe flange
30. Copper joint line

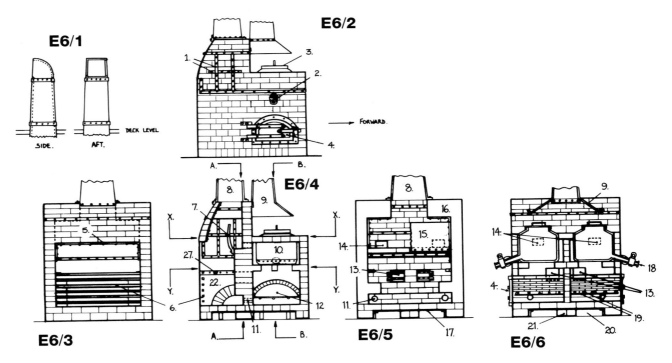

E6/1

E6/2

E6/3

E6/4

E6/5

E6/6

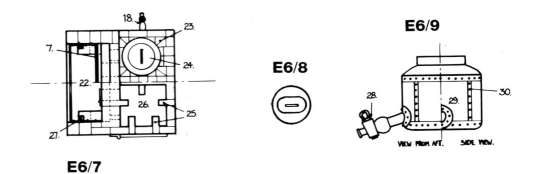

E6/7

E6/8

E6/9

E Fittings

E7

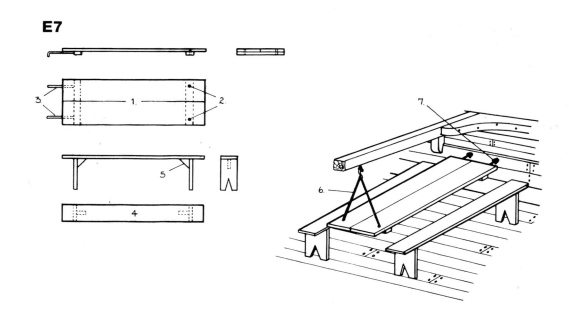

E8/1

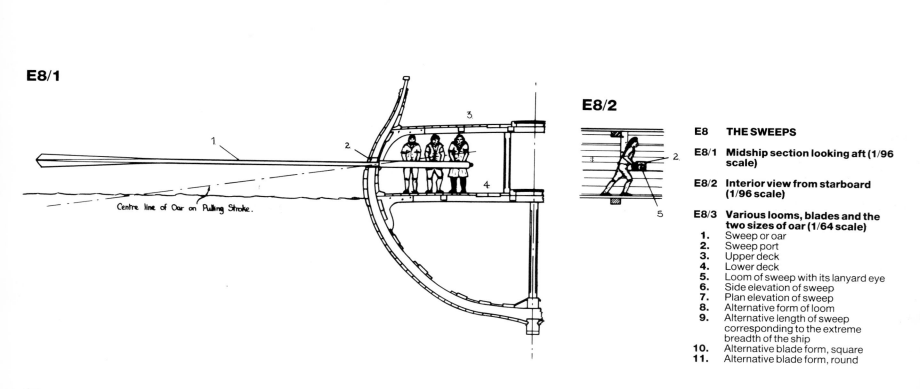

Centre line of Oar on Pulling Stroke.

E8/2

E9 HATCHWAYS AND GRATING DETAILS (1/48 scale)

E9/1 Plan view

E9/2 Longitudinal section

E9/3 Athwartships section

E9/4 Perspective view (no scale)
1. Carling
2. Deck beam
3. Head ledges
4. Coaming
5. Centre ledge
6. Grating frame
7. Grating ledges (same depth as the grating frame)
8. Grating battens (half the depth of the grating ledges)
9. Sill
10. Grating frame
11. Deck planking
12. Recess for the grating ledge
13. Halving joint for grating batten

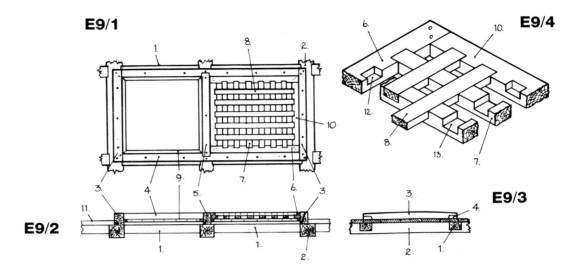

E9/1

E9/4

E9/2

E9/3

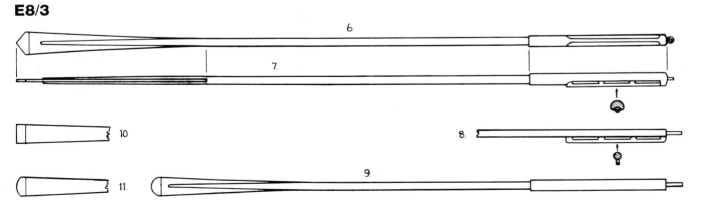

E8/3

85

F Armament

F1/1 **Inboard view of gunport (1/48 scale)**
1. Lead linings for the lead of the gunport lid tackle
2. Eyebolts to secure gun muzzle when lid was shut
3. Inboard sheer rail
4. Gunport
5. Lining (or quickwork)
6. Ringbolts for the gun tackle
7. Ringbolts for the breeching
8. Spirketting

F1/2 **Section through gunport (number 10) (1/48 scale)**
1. Lead lining for the lead of the gunport tackle
2. Gunport tackle halyard
3. Mizzen channel
4. Eyebolt to secure the gun muzzle
5. Ringbolt for gunport lid halyard
6. Gunport lid
7. Ringbolt for closing the lid and securing shut
8. Ship's side planking
9. Lining (or quickwork)
10. Ringbolt for the gun tackle
11. Ringbolt for the breeching
12. Clenching of the ringbolts
13. Spirketting
14. Waterway
15. Upper deck

F1/3 **External view of lid (1/48 scale)**
1. Hinge pintle
2. Hinge and gudgeon
3. Port lid planking (conforms to the sheer of the ship's side planking)
4. Ringbolts for the halyards

F1/4 **Internal view of lid (1/48 scale)**
1. Vertical stiffening planks
2. Ringbolt for closing and securing lid

F1/5 **Section through sweep port (1/48 scale)**
1. Deck clamp
2. Lining (or quickwork)
3. Black strake (strake above the main wale)
4. Upper strake of the main wale
5. Internal view of sweep port lid
6. End view of sweep port lid
7. External view of sweep port lid
8. Sweep port lid hinge
9. Hinge pintle
10. Securing ringbolt
11. Strake between the wales (filling strake)
12. Lower strake of the main wale
13. Strake below the main wale
14. Timber (or frame)
15. Spirketting

F1/1

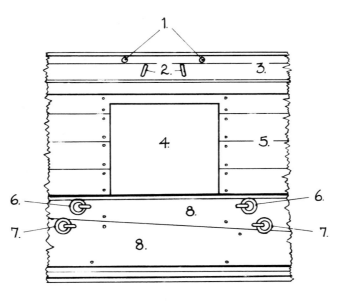

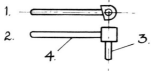

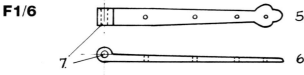

F1/6

F1/7

F1/2

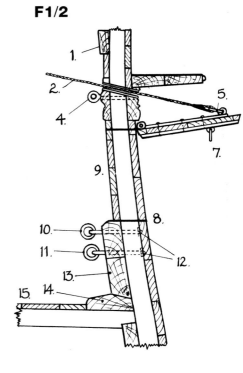

F1/5

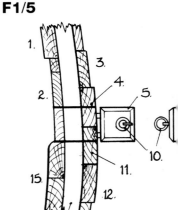

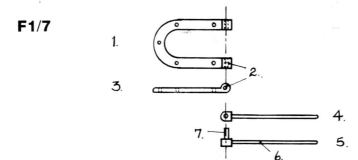

F1/6 **Detail of the gunport lid hinge (1/12 scale)**
1. Side elevation of the pintle
2. Plan of the pintle
3. Pintle (or pin)
4. Securing bolt
5. Plan of the hinge
6. Side elevation of the hinge
7. Gudgeon of the hinge

F1/7 **Detail of the sweep port lid hinge (1/12 scale)**
1. Side elevation of the hinge
2. Gudgeon of the hinge
3. Plan of the hinge
4. Side elevation of the pintle
5. Plan of the pintle
6. Securing bolt
7. Pintle (or pin)

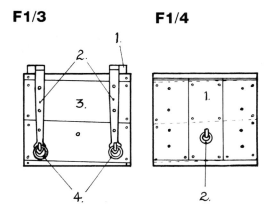

F1/3

F1/4

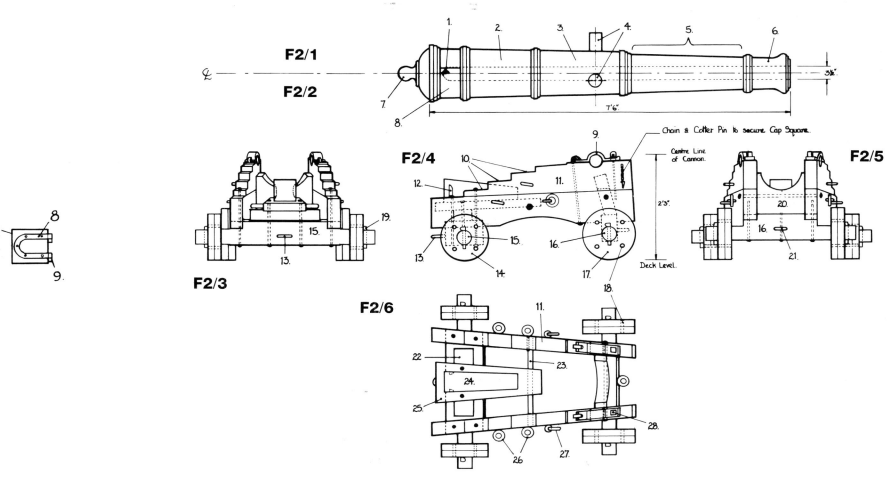

F2 RECONSTRUCTION OF THE
6-POUNDER CARRIAGE GUN AS
AUTHORISED BY THE GUN
ESTABLISHMENT OF 1716 (1/24
scale)
Gun 7ft 6in long, 18 cwt, 3½in bore.
Carriage 4ft 3in long, 3½in thick,
made from elm.
Trucks made from oak.

F2/1 Plan of gun

F2/2 Side elevation of gun

F2/3 Rear elevation of carriage

F2/4 Side elevation of carriage

F2/5 Front elevation of carriage

F2/6 Plan view of carriage
1. The vent or touch hole
2. First reinforce
3. Second reinforce
4. Trunnion
5. Chase
6. Muzzle
7. Cascable

8. Breech
9. Cap square
10. Steps for handspike
11. Carriage cheek
12. Quoin
13. Training tackle ringbolt
14. Rear truck
15. Rear axletree
16. Front axletree
17. Front truck
18. Truck dowels
19. Removable pin
20. Transom
21. Ringbolt
22. Bolster or pig
23. Tie bolt
24. Quoin
25. Bed
26. Ringbolts for the breeching
27. Ring for the gun tackle
28. Cap square retaining bolt

F Armament

F3 GUN TACKLE, SHOT AND
EQUIPMENT (1/96 scale)

F3/1 Side view of the gun run out

F3/2 Plan view of the gun run out

F3/3 Shot

F3/4 Gun tools
  1. Ringbolt
  2. Traversing tackle
  3. Breeching rope
  4. Gun tackle
  5. Eyebolt
  6. Ringbolt
  7. Solid round shot
  8. Chain shot
  9. Bar shot
 10. Expanding shot
 11. Tampion
 12. Ram rod
 13. Sponge
 14. Worm
 15. Flexible rammer and sponge
       combined

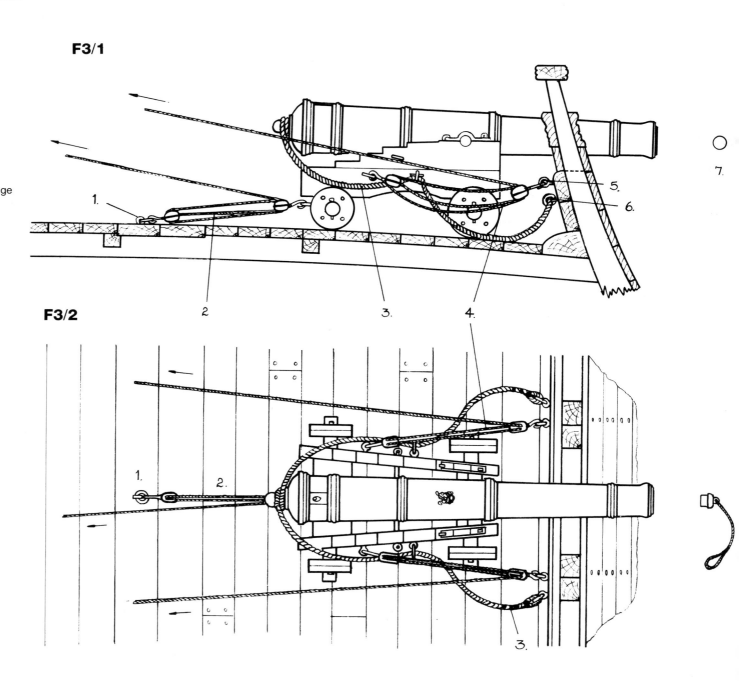

F3/1

F3/2

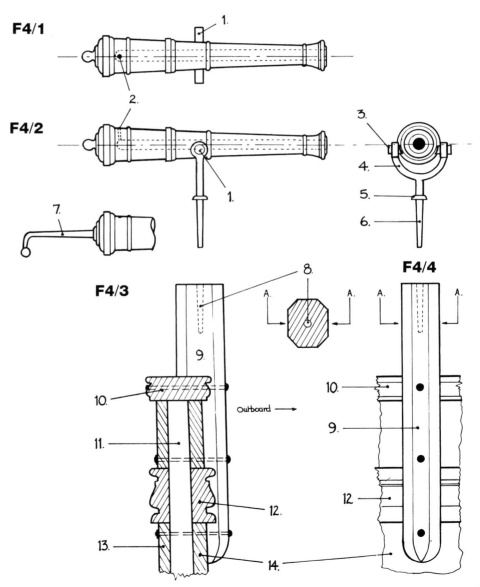

**F4	HALF-POUNDER SWIVEL GUN,**
*c*1720 (1/12 scale)
Weight 3qtrs 18lb

**F4/1	Plan**

**F4/2	Side elevation**

**F4/3	Athwartship section of stock**

F4/4	**Side elevation of stock**
1.	Trunnion
2.	Vent or touch hole
3.	Protruding part of trunnion
4.	Yoke or swivel crutch
5.	Shoulder or stop
6.	Spike or swivel crutch
7.	Alternative type of cascable
8.	Spike hole for swivel crutch
9.	Oak pedestal
10.	Waist rail
11.	Toptimber or frame
12.	Planksheer
13.	Lining planking
14.	Ship's side planking

F3/3

8.	9.	10.

F3/4

12.	13.	14.	15.

F4/1

1.

2.

F4/2

3.

1.

4.

5.

6.

7.

F4/3

8.

9.

10.

11.

12.

13.

Outboard →

F4/4

A.	A.	A.	A.

10.

9.

12.

14.

F5 **13-INCH SEA MORTAR AND SHELL (BOMB) DETAILS (1/48 scale)**

F5/1 **Plan view of mortar**

F5/2 **Plan view of bed**

F5/3 **End elevation from front of bed**

F5/4 **Side elevation of bed**

F5/5 **Side elevation of bed and mortar combined**

F5/6 **Side elevation of mortar**

F5/7 **Details of mortar shell**
1. Vent and pan
2. Shell chamber
3. Charge chamber
4. Trunnion
5. Centre support block
6. Mortar supporter
7. Cap square
8. Spindle for rotation
9. Cross blocks
10. Rotating base
11. Rear transom
12. Bed cheeks
13. Front transom
14. Section of base keyed into bed
15. Lower section of spindle (set into a step)
16. Iron keep plates
17. Reinforcing
18. Shoe for locating the mortar to support
19. Shell, with fuse (the profile and size of solid shot were the same without the fuse and cone)
20. Timing cone
21. Fuse
22. Fuse passing through holes
23. Shell casing
24. Explosive
25. Timing hole for fuse to weave through
26. Tail end of fuse in explosive

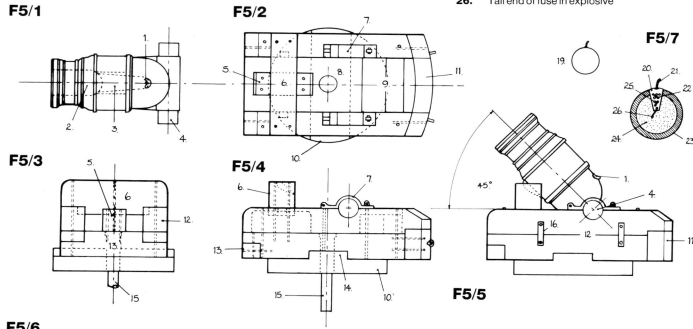

F5/1

F5/2

F5/7

F5/3

F5/4

F5/5

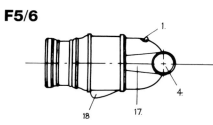

F5/6

G Masts and spars

G1 MASTS AND YARDS (1/192 scale)
1. Ensign staff
2. Mizzen mast
3. Mizzen yard (lateen yard)
4. Crossjack yard
5. Mizzen top
6. Mizzen topsail yard (in lowered position)
7. Mizzen topmast
8. Mizzen topsail yard (in raised position)
9. Pole head of topmast (short stump type, later type was longer)
10. Main mast
11. Main yard
12. Main top
13. Main topsail yard (in lowered position)
14. Main topmast
15. Main topsail yard (in raised position)
16. Main topmast crosstrees
17. Main topgallant yard (in lowered position)
18. Main topgallant mast
19. Main topgallant yard (in raised position)
20. Pole head of topgallant mast (later changed to a royal mast)
21. Fore mast
22. Fore yard
23. Fore top
24. Fore topsail yard (in lowered position)
25. Fore topmast
26. Fore topsail yard (in raised position)
27. Fore topmast crosstrees
28. Fore topgallant yard (in lowered position)
29. Fore topgallant mast
30. Fore topgallant yard (in raised position)
31. Pole head of topgallant mast (later changed to a royal mast)
32. Bowsprit
33. Spritsail yard
34. Jibboom
35. Jack staff

G1

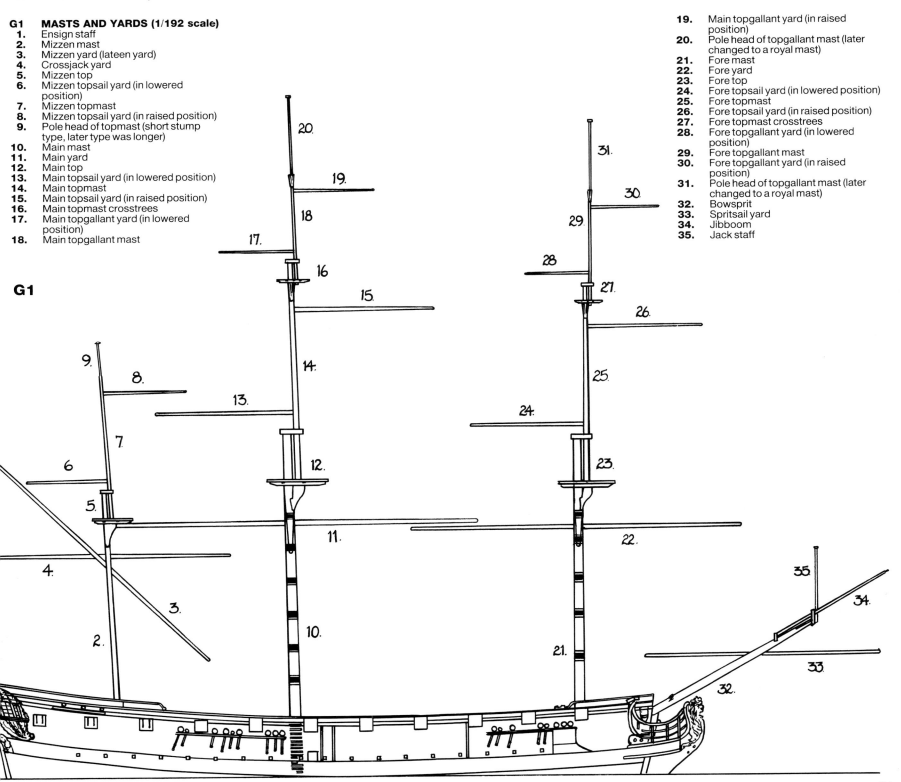

G Masts and spars

G2/1

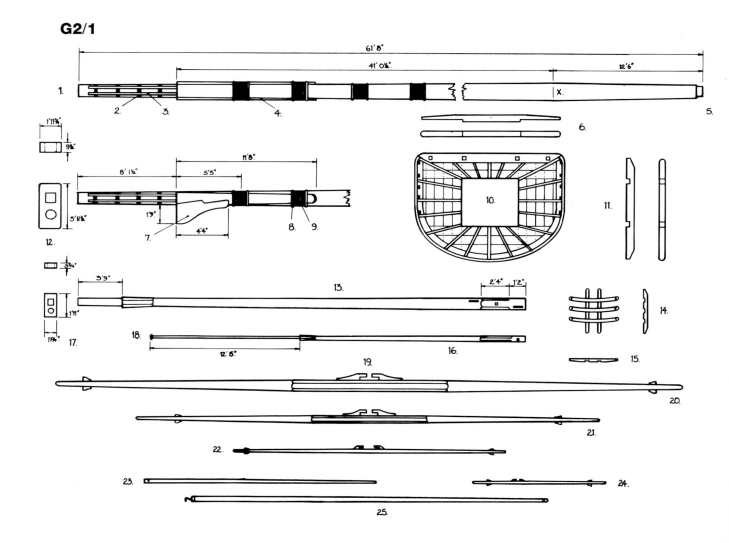

G3 THE MAIN MAST

G3/1 Yards, tops and caps, etc (1/96 scale)

1. Main mast
2. Iron bands
3. Mast head battens
4. Cheeks
5. Bibs
6. Rope woolding
7. Woolding stops
8. Main top
9. Crosstrees
10. Trestletrees
11. Main mast cap
12. Main topmast
13. Topmast trestletrees
14. Topmast crosstrees
15. Topmast cap
16. Main topgallant mast
17. Main royal mast
18. Topsail studdingsail boom
19. Main yard
20. Main topsail yard
21. Studdingsail yard
22. Main topgallant yard
23. Lower studdingsail boom
X. Partners

G3/1

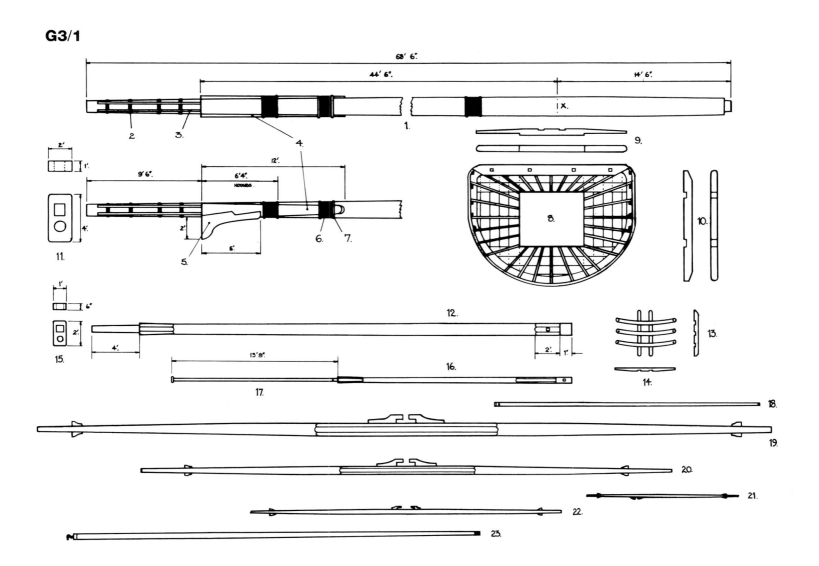

G   Masts and spars

G4   MIZZEN MAST

Note: Rope wooldings were not introduced until 1733, when only three were fitted.

G4/1   Masts, yards, top and cap (1/96 scale)

1. Mizzen mast
2. Bibs
3. Crosstrees
4. Mizzen top
5. Trestletrees
6. Mizzen mast cap
7. Mizzen topmast
8. Crossjack yard
9. Plan elevation of mizzen yard (lateen yard)
10. Side elevation of yardarm
11. Mizzen topsail yard
X. Partners

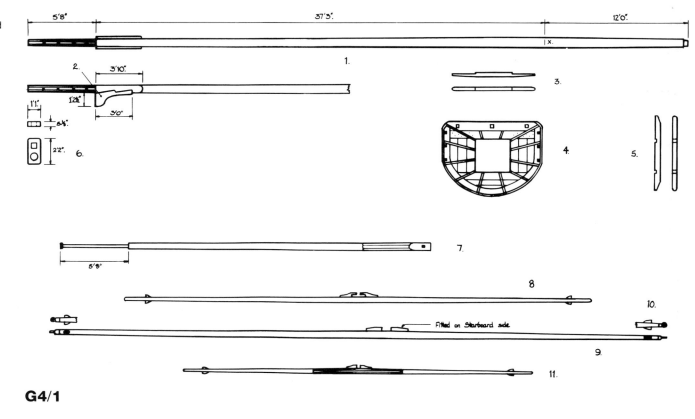

G4/1

G5   BOWSPRIT, JIBBOOM AND SPRITSAIL YARD (1/96 scale)

G5/1   Bowsprit

G5/2   Jibboom

G5/3   Bowsprit cap

G5/4   Spritsail yard

1. Gammoning cleats
2. Spritsail yard sling cleat or stop
3. Stop or heel for the jibboom
4. Bee blocks
5. The bees
6. Slot for the jack staff
7. Sling cleats

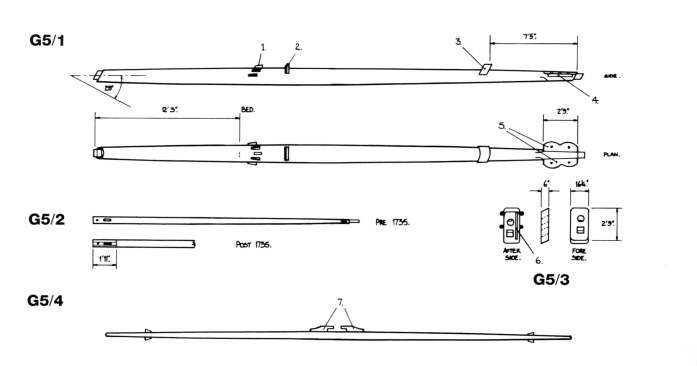

G5/1

G5/2

G5/3

G5/4

G6   MAIN TOP AND MAST CAP (1/96 scale)

G6/1   Section

G6/2   Athwartships section

G6/3   Crosstrees and trestletrees from above

G6/4   Plan view of the top

G6/5   Planking of the top
1. Mast cap
2. Main topmast
3. Head of the main mast
4. Bolster
5. Iron fid
6. Battens
7. Rim of the top
8. Trestletrees
9. Bibs
10. Cheeks
11. Crosstrees
12. Rail
13. Slots for the topmast deadeye plates
14. Lubber's hole
15. Planking of the top
16. Iron plate for the fid to rest upon
17. Fore and aft planking of the top
18. Athwartships planking of the top
19. Halving joint for the top planking

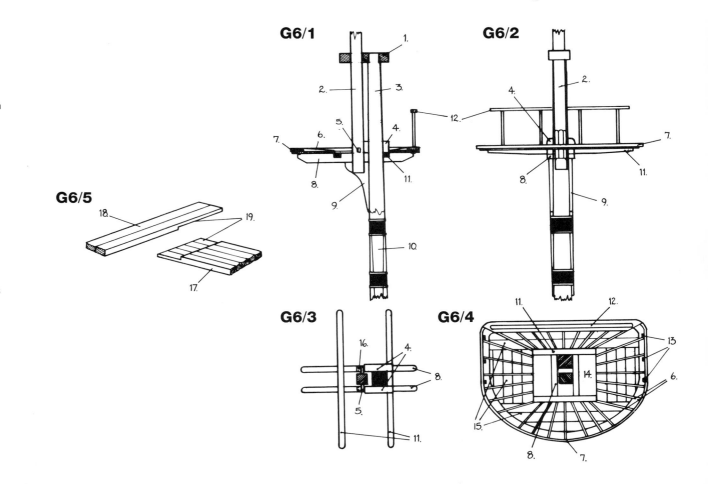

G7   Flagstaffs and boomkins (1/96 scale)
1. Ensign staff
2. Halyard cleat
3. Heel
4. Jack staff
5. Retaining brackets
6. Bowsprit cap
7. Plan view of square type boomkin
8. Side elevation of the square section boomkin
9. Timberhead stop for tack lead block
10. Plan view of curved type of boomkin
11. Side elevation of curved type of boomkin
12. Sheave slot
13. Octagonal section
14. Round section

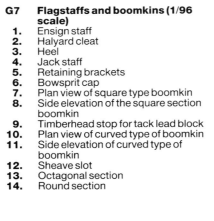

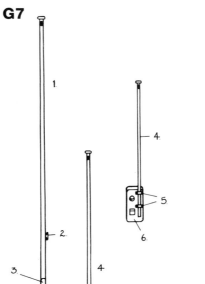

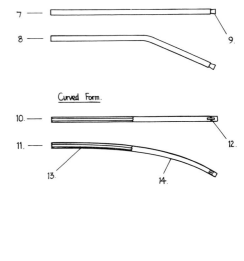

Curved Form.

H Rigging

H1 STANDING RIGGING

H1/1 Stays and backstays (1/192 scale)
1. Fore topgallant stay
2. Fore topmast stay
3. Fore top crowsfeet
4. Fore preventer stay
5. Fore stay
6. Fore stay and preventer stay hearts
7. Fore topmast stay tackle
8. Main stay hearts
9. Main stay collar
10. Bobstay
11. Bowsprit shroud
12. Main topgallant stay
13. Fore topgallant backstay
14. Main topmast stay
15. Fore topmast backstay
16. Main top crowsfeet
17. Main hatch tackle
18. Main preventer stay
19. Preventer stay deadeyes
20. Main stay
21. Fore hatch tackle
22. Fore backstay stool and deadeyes
23. Main topgallant backstay
24. Mizzen topmast stay
25. Mizzen topmast stay deadeyes
26. Mizzen top crowsfeet
27. Main topmast backstay
28. Mizzen stay
29. Mizzen stay deadeyes
30. Main backstay stool and deadeyes
31. Mizzen topmast back stay deadeyes
32. Mizzen topmast backstay

H1/1

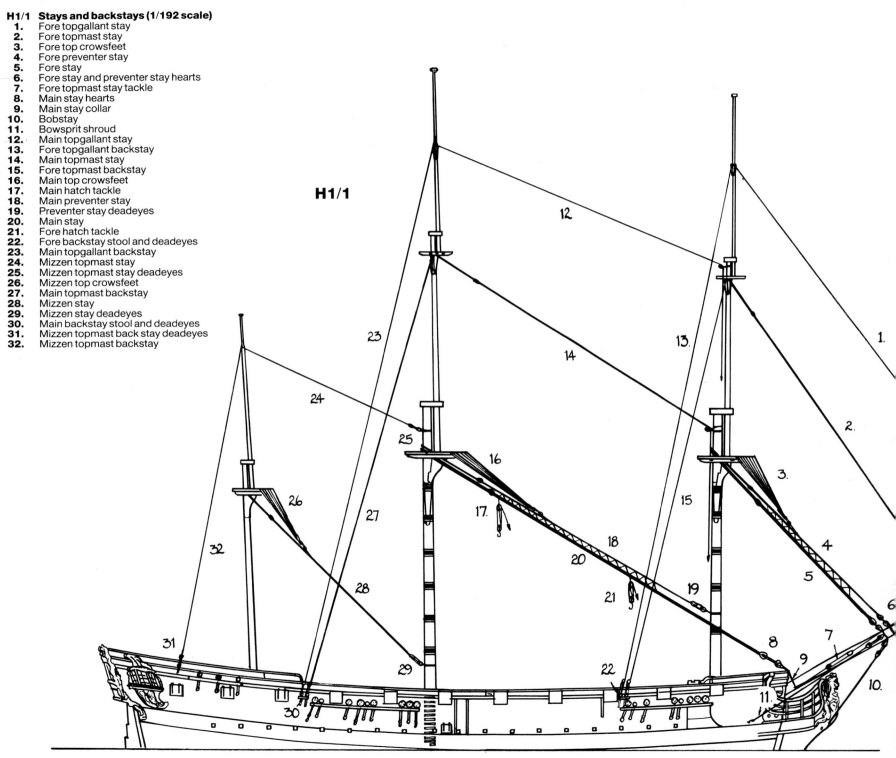

H1/2

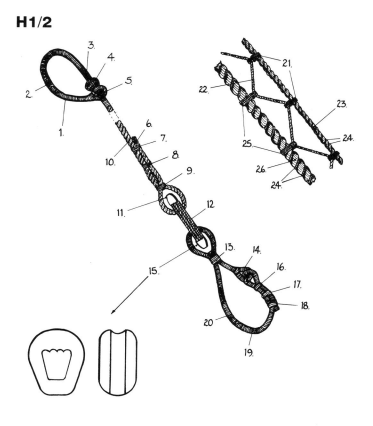

H Rigging

H1/3 Shrouds and ratlines (1/192 scale)
1. Bobstay (1)
2. Bowsprit shrouds (1 each side)
3. Fore topgallant shrouds (2 each side)
4. Fore topgallant backstay (1 each side)
5. Fore topmast futtock shrouds (2 each side)
6. Fore topmast shrouds (3 each side)
7. Fore topmast backstay (1 each side)
8. Fore topmast deadeyes
9. Fore futtock shrouds (3 each side)
10. Fore shrouds (6 each side)
11. Fore shroud deadeyes
12. Ratlines
13. Fore backstay stool
14. Main topgallant shrouds (2 each side)
15. Main topgallant backstay (1 each side)
16. Main topmast futtock shrouds (2 each side)
17. Main topmast backstay (1 each side)
18. Main topmast shrouds (3 each side)
19. Main topmast deadeyes
20. Main futtock shrouds (3 each side)
21. Main shrouds (7 each side)
22. Main shroud deadeyes
23. Main backstay stool
24. Mizzen topmast shrouds (2 each side)
25. Mizzen topmast backstay (1 each side)
26. Mizzen topmast deadeyes
27. Mizzen futtock shrouds (2 each sde)
28. Mizzen shrouds (3 each side)
29. Mizzen shroud deadeyes
30. Mizzen backstay deadeyes

H1/4 Lower shrouds of the main mast (1/96 scale)
1. Main topgallant mast backstay
2. Main topmast backstay
3. Main backstay
4—9 Main shrouds
10. Ratlines
11. Shroud batten
12. Backstay stool
13. Channel knee
14. Deadeye lanyards
15. Upper deadeye
16. Lower deadeye
17. Main channel
18. Chain plates
19. Slots for the chain plates
20. Line of the hull planking

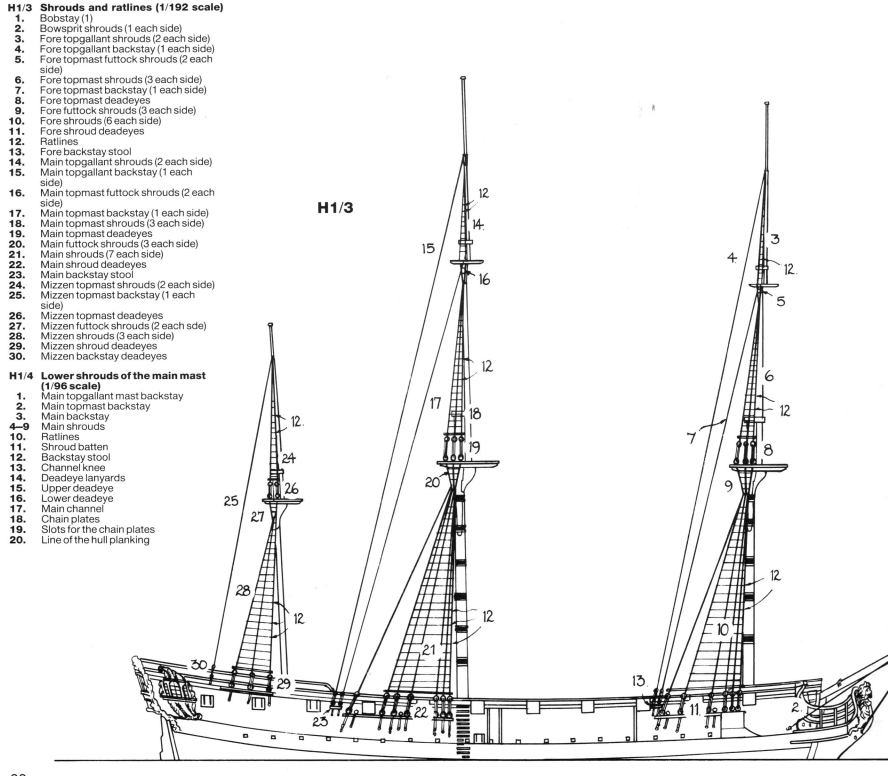

H1/3

H1/4

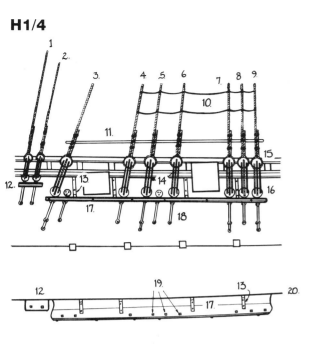

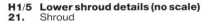

H1/5

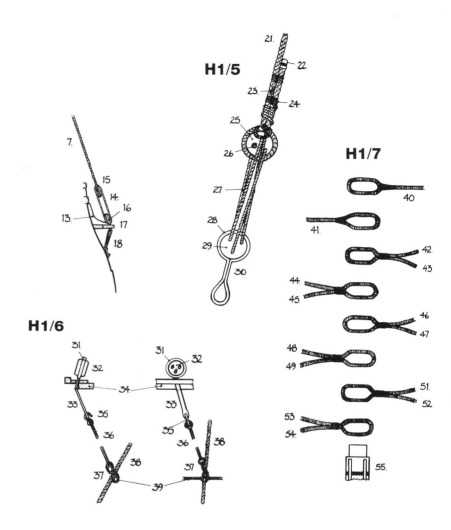

H1/6

H1/7

H1/8

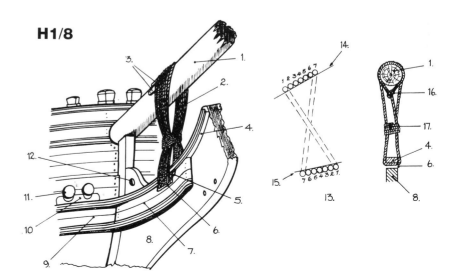

H1/5 Lower shroud details (no scale)
21. Shroud
22. Canvas cover over shroud tail end
23. Loose end of lanyard, seized to shroud
24. Shroud seizing
25. Upper deadeye
26. Monkey fist end of lanyard
27. Deadeye lanyard
28. Iron chain
29. Lower deadeye
30. Clenched part of the chain

H1/6 Futtock shrouds (no scale)
31. Chain
32. Lower deadeye of the topmast shrouds
33. Chain plate
34. Main top rim
35. Futtock shroud hook
36. Futtock shroud
37. Eye and seizing of the futtock shroud
38. Main shroud
39. Futtock shroud stave

H1/7 Disposition of the main shroud eyes at the mast head (no scale)
40. Larboard (port) main backstay
41. Starboard main backstay
42. No 6 port shroud
43. No 5 port shroud
44. No 6 starboard shroud
45. No 5 starboard shroud
46. No 4 port shroud
47. No 3 port shroud
48. No 4 starboard shroud
49. No 3 starboard shroud
50. No 2 port shroud
51. No 1 port shroud
52. No 2 starboard shroud
53. No 1 starboard shroud
54. Main mast head

H1/8 The gammon lashing (no scale)
1. Bowsprit
2. Gammon lashing
3. Gammon cleats
4. Hair bracket
5. Hardwood wedge
6. Slot for the gammon lashing
7. Trailboard
8. Knee of the head
9. Cheek
10. Bolster
11. Hawse holes
12. Hole for the main stay collar
13. Manner in which the gammon lashing was rove. The numbers depict the order of the turns
14. Line of the top surface of the bowsprit
15. Line of the upper edge of the slot
16. Eye spliced in one end of lashing
17. End of lashing seized in place

H Rigging

H2 RUNNING RIGGING OF THE FORE MAST (no scale)

H2/1 View from aft

H2/2 Side view

1. Topgallant lift
2. Foot rope
3. Topgallant clewline
4. Topgallant mast shroud
5. Topsail lift
6. Reef tackle fall blocks
7. Foot rope
8. Reef tackle falls
9. Topmast shrouds
10. Long tackle block
11. Topsail clewlines
12. Fore course reef tackle blocks (long tackle block)
13. Fore yard lifts
14. Yard tackle outer tricing line
15. Futtock shroud
16. Yard tackle pendant
17. Yard tackle
18. Yard tackle inner tricing line
19. Foot rope and stirrups
20. Reef tackle falls
21. Fore mast shroud
22. Fore course clewline
23. Fore mast shroud deadeyes
24. Main topgallant stay
25. Topgallant brace pendant
26. Standing part of brace
27. Running part of brace
28. Brace tackle pendants
29. Topgallant sail bridle
30. Standing part of topsail yard brace
31. Brace pendant
32. Running part of topsail yard brace
33. Brace tackle pendants
34. Main topmast stay
35. Fore topgallant mast stay
36. Fore topsail bridle
37. Topgallant sail bowline
38. Main preventer stay
39. Standing part of the brace
40. Brace pendants
41. Fore topmast stay
42. Topsail bowline
43. Main stay
44. Fore course brace tackle pendants
45. Running part of the brace
46. Fore course bridle
47. Fore course bowline
48. Fore course tack
49. Running part of the fore sheet
50. Standing part of the fore sheet

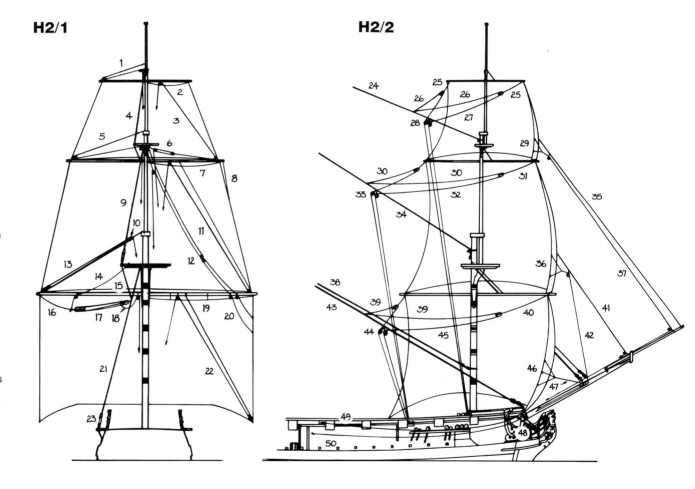

H2/1   H2/2

H3/1 View from aft

H3/2 Side view
1. Topgallant lift
2. Foot rope
3. Topgallant clewline
4. Topgallant mast shroud
5. Topsail reef tackle fall blocks
6. Topsail yard lift
7. Foot rope
8. Reef tackle fall
9. Main topmast shrouds
10. Topsail clewline
11. Long tackle block
12. Main yard lifts
13. Reef tackle fall blocks (long tackle block)
14. Yard tackle outer tricing line
15. Futtock shrouds
16. Tackle pendant
17. Yard tackle
18. Yard tackle inner tricing line
19. Foot rope and stirrups
20. Main course reef tackle falls
21. Main course clewline
22. Main shrouds
23. Main shroud deadeyes
24. Topgallant sail yard brace pendants
25. Standing part of brace
26. Running part of brace
27. Topgallant sail bridle
28. Topgallant mast stay
29. Topgallant sail bowline
30. Topsail yard brace pendant
31. Topmast stay
32. Bowline tackle
33. Bowline tackle pendant to fore topmast
34. Topgallant brace tackle pendants
35. Mizzen topmast stay
36. Standing part of brace
37. Running part of brace
38. Topsail bridle
39. Topsail bowline
40. Topsail brace tackle pendant
41. Brace pendant
42. Standing part of brace
43. Running part of brace
44. Main and preventer stays
45. Main course bridle
46. Main course bowline
47. Standing part of main tack
48. Running part of main tack
49. Standing part of main sheet
50. Running part of main sheet

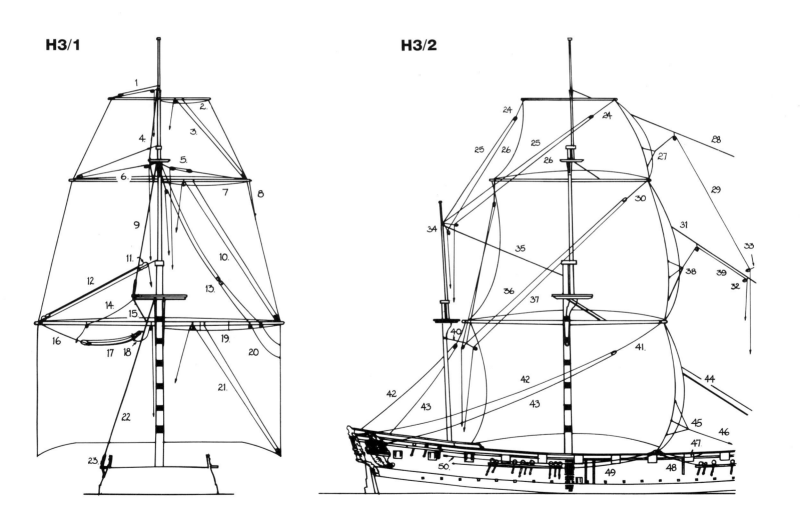

H3/1

H3/2

H4/1

H4/2

H4/3

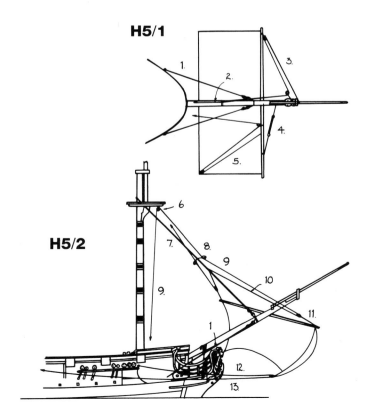

H4	**THE RUNNING RIGGING OF THE MIZZEN MAST (no scale)**

H4/1 Port side view with mizzen set

H4/2 View from aft

H4/3 Starboard side view
1. Mizzen yard lift
2. Standing jeer block
3. Jeer block
4. Aftermost main shroud
5. Peak and throat brails
6. Foot brails
7. Jeer halyard
8. Mizzen sheets
9. Mizzen topmast lift
10. Reef tackle fall blocks
11. Reef tackle falls
12. Foot rope
13. Mizzen topmast shrouds
14. Topsail clewlines
15. Crossjack lifts
16. Mizzen futtock shrouds
17. Foot rope and stirrups
18. Mizzen shrouds
19. Mizzen shroud deadeyes
20. Topsail brace pendant
21. Mizzen topmast stay
22. Standing part of topsail brace
23. Running part of topsail brace
24. Topsail bridle
25. Topsail bowline
26. Main topmast back stay
27. Crossjack brace pendant
28. Standing part of crossjack brace
29. Running part of crossjack brace
30. Mizzen bowline
31. Mizzen topsail brace block pendants

H5	**THE RUNNING RIGGING OF THE SPRITSAIL (no scale)**

H5/1 Plan view

H5/2 Side view
1. Bowsprit shroud
2. Fall of the spritsail yard lift
3. Spritsail lift
4. Standing lift
5. Clewline
6. Brace block
7. Fore stay
8. Pendant blocks
9. Fall and running part of the brace
10. Standing part of the brace
11. Brace block and pendant
12. Standing part of the spritsail sheet
13. Running part of the spritsail sheet

H5/1

H5/2

H6 YARDARM FITTINGS AND RIGGING

H6/1 Stunsail boom and yardarm (1/24 scale)
1. Upper stunsail boom
2. Lower yard
3. Yardarm cleat
4. Outer stunsail boom iron
5. Inner stunsail boom iron
6. Boom iron yoke
7. Retaining hoops

H6/2 Boom iron hoops (1/24 scale)
1. Outer stunsail boom iron hoop
2. Hoop around yardarm
3. Boom iron yoke
4. Inner stunsail boom iron hoop
5. Hoop around yard

H6/3 Plan view of yardarm (1/24 scale)
1. Yardarm
2. Yardarm cleat

H6/4 Yardarm and brace pendant (no scale)
1. Yardarm cleat
2. Yardarm
3. Brace pendant
4. Brace block
5. Running part of the brace

H6/5 Lower mast cap (no scale)
1. Lower mast cap
2. Long tackle pendant
3. Fall of the lift
4. Long tackle block
5. Running part of the lift

H6/6 Yardarm and associated blocks (no scale)
1. Running part of the lift
2. Single block seized to topsail sheet block
3. Standing part of the lift
4. Lift and sheet block strop
5. Yardarm
6. Topsail sheet block
7. Yardarm cleat
8. Strop for standing part of lift

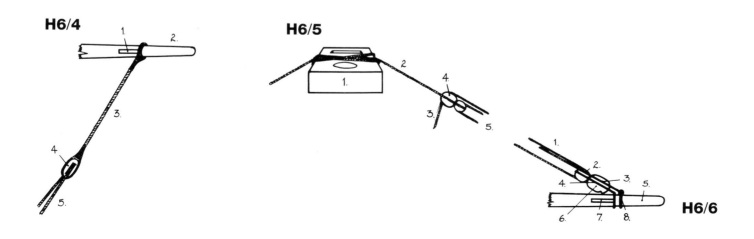

H   Rigging

H7   ARRANGEMENT OF THE YARD BLOCKS (no scale)

Note This entry applies to the fore mast and mizzen mast yards. However, no stunsails were fitted on the mizzen mast and foot ropes were not always fitted on the crossjack yard.

H7/1   Main yard

H7/2   Topsail yard

H7/3   Topgallant yard
1. Main yard
2. Jeer blocks
3. Sling cleat
4. Quarter block for horses (foot ropes)
5. Lower stunsail inner halyard block
6. Buntline block
7. Clewline block
8. Buntline block
9. Block for the tricing line
10. Inner stunsail boom iron
11. Horse block
12. Lower stunsail inner halyard block
13. Main yard lift block
14. Main topsail sheet block
15. Outer stunsail boom iron
16. Main brace block
17. Yard tackle

18. Topsail yard
19. Tie block
20. Sling cleat
21. Clewline block
22. Buntline block
23. Topsail yard lift block
24. Brace block
25. Stunsail yard boom iron
26. Jewel block for the topmast stunsail halyard
27. Topgallant yard
28. Sling cleats
29. Clewline block
30. Brace block
31. Topgallant yard lift block
32. Jewel block for topgallant stunsail yard halyard (if fitted)

H8   METHOD OF SCARPHING THE YARDS (no scale)
1. Side elevation showing scarph face of one half of the yard
2. Plan of one half of the yard
3. Plan of opposite half of the yard
4. Dowel (or coak) holes, adjoining the two portions of the opposite.

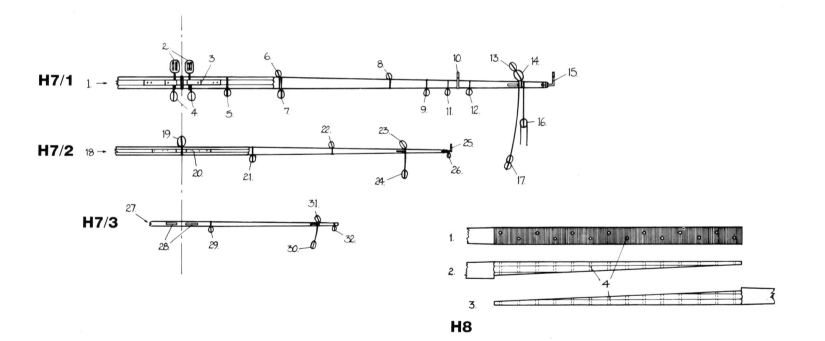

104

H9 **JEERS AND TIES (no scale)**
Note The yards of the other masts were rigged in a similar manner except for the mizzen topsail yard which was rigged as a topgallant yard.

H9/1 **Main yard viewed from forward**

H9/2 **Main yard viewed from side**

H9/3 **Main topsail yard viewed from forward**

H9/4 **Main topsail yard viewed from side**

H9/5 **Main topgallant yard viewed from forward**

H9/6 **Main topgallant yard viewed from side**
1. Masthead cleat
2. Lashing for the jeer strop
3. Crosstrees
4. Jeer strop
5. Tresstletree
6. Jeer block (double)
7. Jeer tackle
8. Main yard
9. Lower jeer block (double)
10. Yard sling cleat
11. Fall of the jeers
12. Main mast
13. Tie pendants
14. Topmast crosstree
15. Standing tie block (single
16. Single tie block
17. Main topsail yard
18. Falls of the ties
19. Main topmast
20. Topmast trestletree
21. Yard sling cleat
22. Tie sheave set into masthead
23. Tie
24. Yard sling cleat
25. Topgallant mast

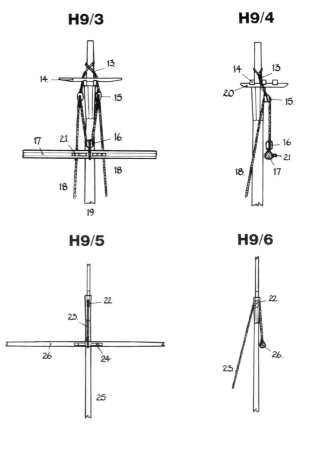

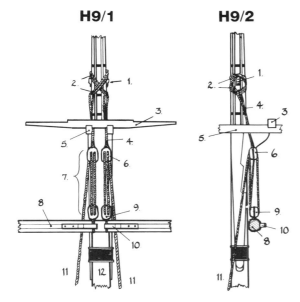

H Rigging

H10   YARD PARRELS AND SLINGS (no scale)

H10/1 General arrangement
1. Mast
2. Yard
3. Sling
4. Thimble (seized to sling)
5. Parrel rib
6. Parrel truck
7. Fall of the parrel rope
8. End of the parrel rope seized to fall
9. Eyes of the parrel rope (to pass around yard)
10. Rose lashing

H10/2 Spritsail yard
1. Sling
2. Bowsprit
3. Spritsail yard
4. Saddle
5. Leather pad (apron)
6. Halyard sling

H10/3 Mizzen yard
1. Parrel rope
2. Parrel truck
3. Parrel rib
4. Thimble (seized to sling)
5. Jeer block
6. Mizzen yard
7. Mizzen mast
8. Seizing of the end of the parrel rope to fall
9. Sling
10. Fall of the parrel rope

H10/1

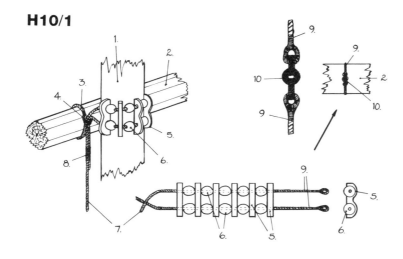

H10/3

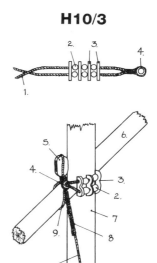

H10/2

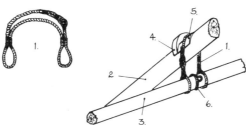

1. Main topmast
2. Main mast cap
3. Mizzen topmast stay
4. Mizzen topmast stay lead block
5. Main topmast shrouds
6. Strops for the jeer pendants
7. Mast head cleat
8. Ratlines
9. Jeer block pendant
10. Main topmast shroud deadeyes
11. Main top rim
12. Main top capping
13. Long tackle block for the main yard lifts
14. Deadeyes
15. Main top rail
16. Main topmast shroud lanyards
17. Eyes of the lower mast shrouds
18. Bolsters
19. Crosstrees
20. Trestletrees
21. Boarding of the top
22. Battens
23. Main yard lift
24. Deadeye plates
25. Buntline block
26. Crowsfoot eyeholes
27. Futtock shroud hooks
28. Toggles securing buntline blocks
29. Futtock shrouds
30. Jeer block
31. Jeer tackle
32. Mast woolding and hoops
33. Shroud stave
34. Fall of the main yard lift
35. Clewline block
36. Lower stunsail halliard block
37. Yard parral
38. Main shrouds
39. Crowsfeet
40. Main preventer stay
41. Main stay
42. Sling cleat
43. Fall of the main yard lift
44. Mainmast
45. Main yard
46. Euphroe for the crowsfeet
47. Worming of the stay
48. Crowsfeet tensioning tackle
49. Snaking of the stays
50. Jeer fall pendants
51. Standing part of clewline

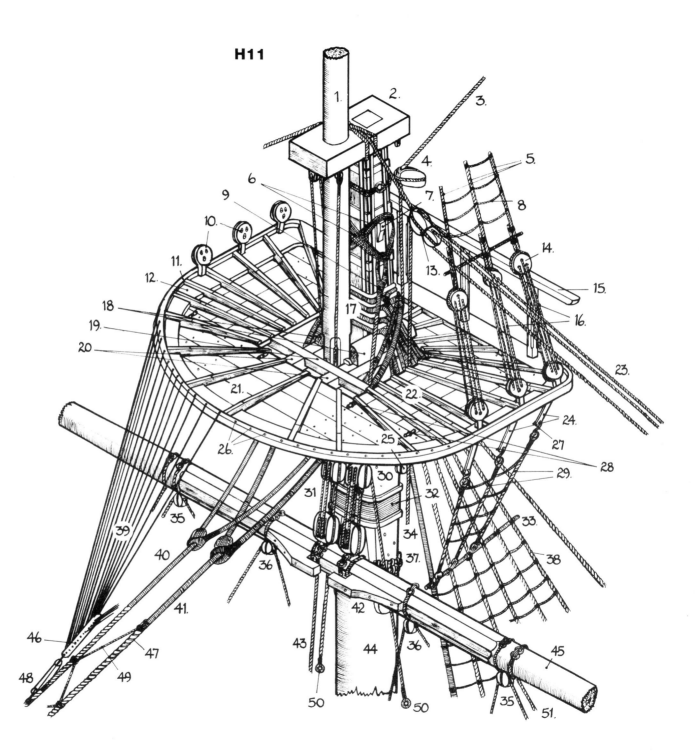

H11

107

H12 DETAIL OF THE FORE TOPMAST HEAD (no scale)

1. Fore topgallant mast
2. Main topgallant stay
3. Main topgallant staysail stay
4. Fore topgallant shrouds and ratlines
5. Fore topmast cap
6. Main topgallant staysail downhauler block
7. Lift block (halyard) pendant
8. Lift halyard block
9. Standing part of the fore topsail yard lift
10. Running part of the fore topsail yard lift
11. Fore topsail yard lift block
12. Fore topsail reef tackle outer block
13. Jewel block for the topmast stunsail halyard
14. Fore topsail reef tackle
15. Fore topsail yard brace pendant
16. Fore topsail yard brace block
17. Running part of the fore topsail yard brace
18. Standing part of the fore topsail yard brace
19. Outer topsail buntline block
20. Reef tackle lead
21. Reef tackle blocks and tackle
22. Inner topsail buntline blocks
23. Standing tie blocks for the topsail yard
24. Tie block of the topsail yard
25. Fore topgallant sail inner sheet block
26. Fore topsail clewline block
27. Standing part of the clewline
28. Running part of the clewline
29. Fore topmast stay
30. Fore topsail clewline fall
31. Fore topgallant sail sheet fall
32. Topsail reef tackle fall
33. Topsail yard lift fall
34. Fore topmast
35. Topsail yard tie fall (only one side shown for clarity)
36. Fore topmast shrouds, 3 in total (one side only shown for clarity)
37. Ratlines
38. Fore topmast standing backstay
39. Fore topgallant sail sheet
40. Fore topsail yard

H12

I Sails

I1 **SQUARE SAILS OF THE FORE MAST (1/192 scale)**
The fore side of the sail is shown on the left, the after side on the right

I1/1 **Fore topsail**

I1/2 **Fore topgallant**

I1/3 **Fore course**

I1/4 **Detail of securing sail to yard (no scale)**
1. Earing
2. Head bolt rope
3. Reef linings
4. Reef cringles
5. Leechline cringles
6. Leech bolt rope
7. Bowline and bridle cringles
8. Top lining
9. Clew
10. Middle band lining
11. Clewline lining
12. Clew cringles
13. Foot bolt rope
14. Sail cloth seam
15. Robband gaskets
16. Leech lining
17. Head lining
18. Robbands
19. Head bolt rope
20. Yard
21. Head seam
22. Robband gaskets
23. Sail cloths
24. Sail cloth seams

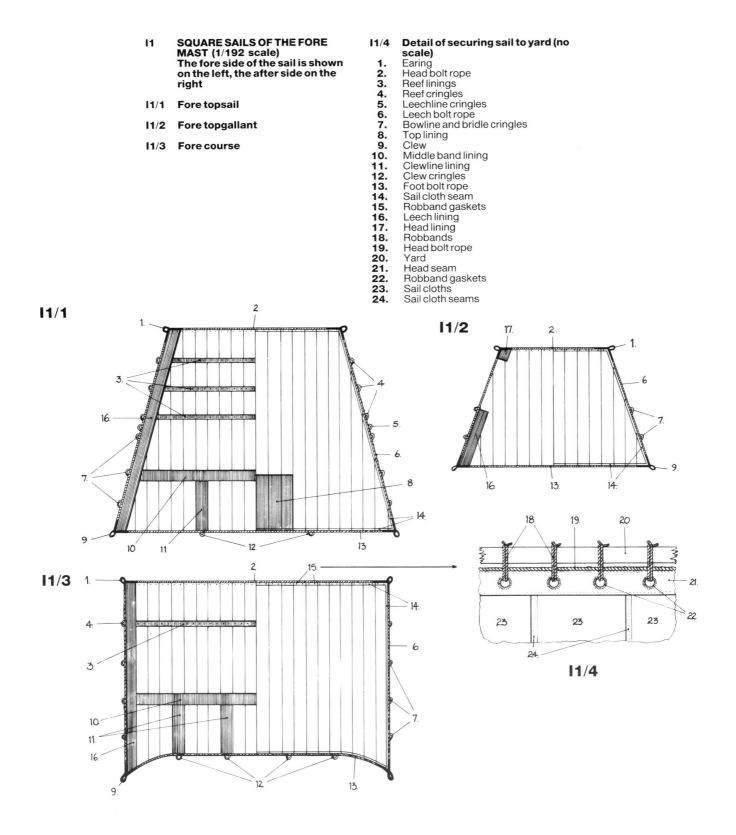

I Sails

I2 THE SQUARE SAILS OF THE MAIN MAST (1/192 scale)
The fore side of the sail is shown to the left, the after side to the right

I2/1 Main topsail

I2/2 Main topgallant

I2/3 Main course

I2/4 Main course clue (no scale)

I2/5 Main topsail and topgallant clew (no scale)

1. Earing
2. Robband gaskets
3. Head bolt rope
4. Seams
5. Leech bolt rope
6. Reef cringles
7. Reef linings
8. Leechline cringle
9. Leech lining
10. Bowline and bridle cringles
11. Middle band lining
12. Clew
13. Clewline lining
14. Clewline cringles

15. Top lining
16. Foot bolt rope
17. Sail cloth
18. Standing part of clewline
19. Running part of clewline
20. Clew block
21. Clew block strop
22. Sheet block strop
23. Tack
24. Eye of the clew around the tack
25. Monkey fist end of tack
26. Standing part of the sheet
27. Running part of the sheet
28. Sheet block
29. Topsail or topgallant sail tack

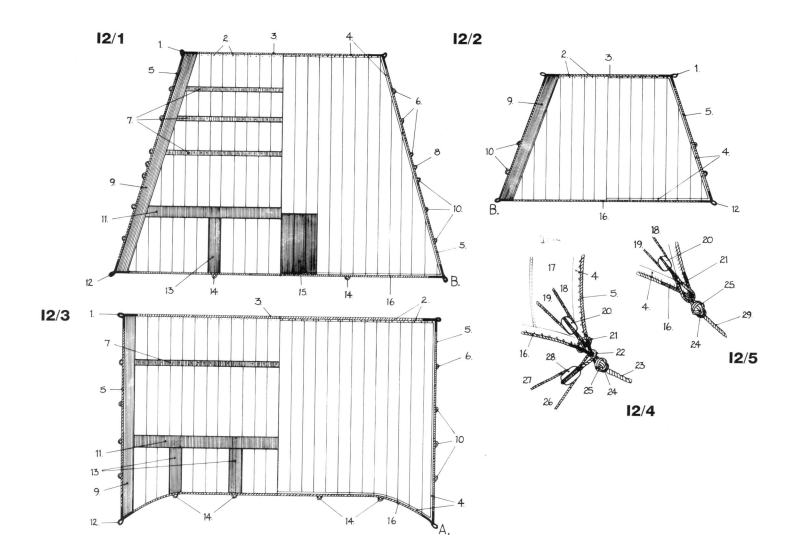

I3   MIZZEN SAILS, SPRITSAIL AND DETAILS

I3/1   Mizzen topsail (1/192 scale)

I3/2   Spritsail (1/192 scale)

I3/3   Mizzen sail (1/192 scale)
1. Head bolt rope
2. Earing
3. Reef cringles
4. Reef band linings
5. Middle band lining
6. Leechline cringle
7. Bowline and bridle cringles
8. Leech lining
9. Seams
10. Clew
11. Top lining
12. Foot bolt rope
13. Leech bolt rope
14. Water hole
15. Brail cringles
16. Leech bolt rope
17. Sheet cringle
18. Foot brail cringle
19. Tack cringle
20. Luff tackle cringle

I3/4   Triple bowline and bridle (no scale)
1. Leech bolt rope
2. Sail cloth seam
3. Sail cloth
4. Cringle

I3/5   Detail of a cringle (no scale)
1. Cringle
2. Bolt rope
3. Sail cloth seam

I3/6   Double bowline and bridle (no scale)
1. Leech bolt rope
2. Sail cloth seam
3. Sail cloth
4. Cringle

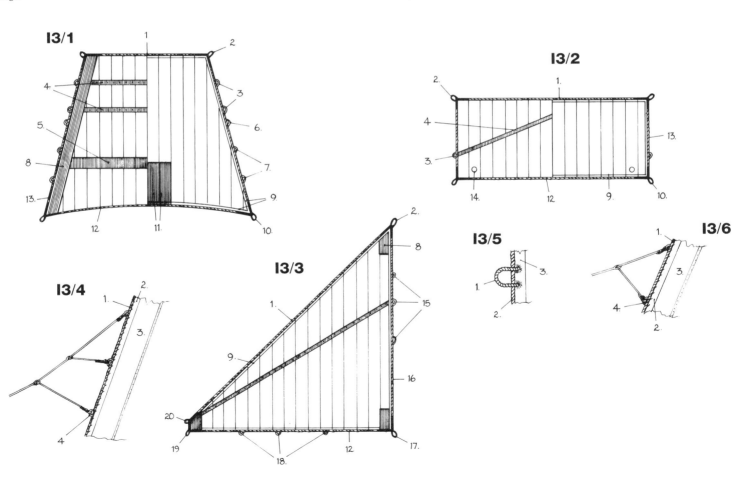

I Sails

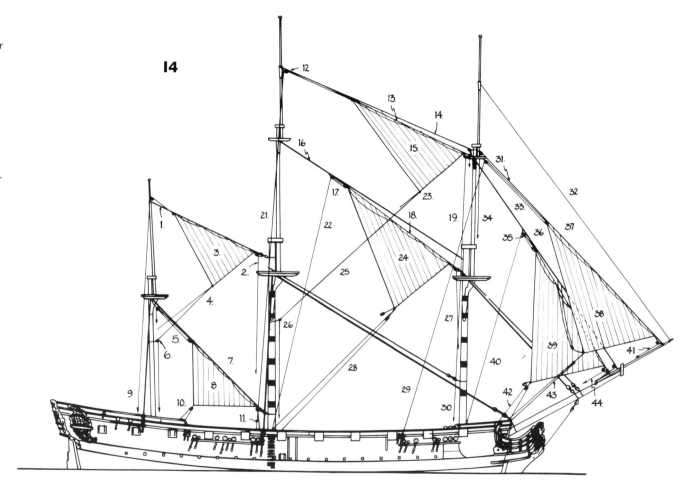

I4

I5 FORE AND AFT SAILS (Port side only shown to reveal lining details; 1/192 scale)

I5/1 Jibsail

I5/2 Main topgallant staysail

I5/3 Mizzen topmast staysail

I5/4 Mizzen staysail

I5/5 Fore topmast staysail

I5/6 Main topmast staysail

I5/7 Detail of staysail stay (main topgallant staysail)

1. Luff bolt rope
2. Peak and its lining
3. Leech bolt rope
4. Clew and its lining
5. Tack and its lining
6. Foot bolt rope
7. Halyard earing
8. Clew lining
9. Leech bolt rope
10. Seam
11. Tack cringle
12. Clew
13. Halyard block
14. Seizing of the staysail stay to the topgallant stay
15. Fall of the halyard
16. Topgallant stay
17. Robbands
18. Staysail stay
19. Downhauler
20. Thimble for downhauler
21. Tack block pendant
22. Thimble for staysail stay fastened to fore topmast head
23. Downhauler block seized to bolt rope
24. Tack block
25. Downhauler fall
26. Tack
27. Fall of the staysail stay secured to fore top
28. Sheets fitted to clew with a thimble

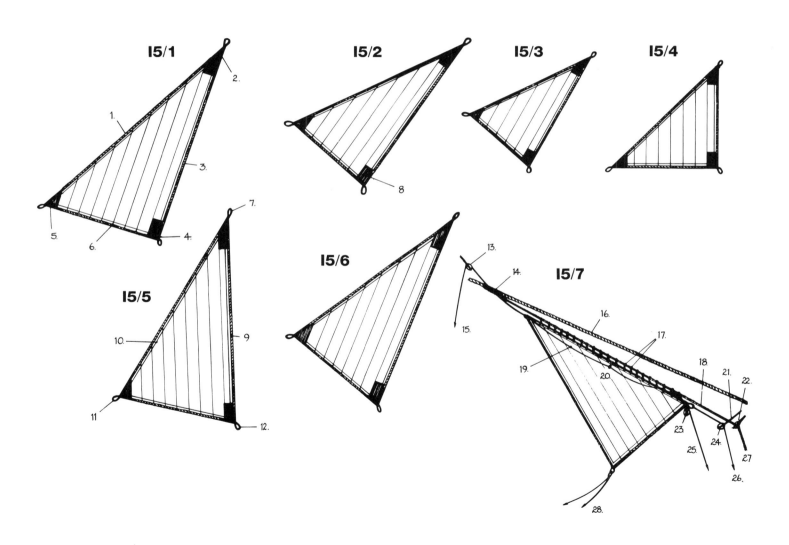

I Sails

I6   **MAIN LOWER AND TOPMAST STUDDING SAILS (no scale)**
Note   Fore mast rigged in the same way

I6/1   **The rigging of the lower studding sail**
1.   Main topmast
2.   Outer halyard block
3.   Outer halyard
4.   Topmast stunsail sheet block
5.   Main stunsail boom
6.   Main stunsail yard
7.   Main yard
8.   Inner halyard
9.   Topping lift
10.   Brace
11.   Main lower stunsail
12.   Main mast
13.   Main course
14.   Tacks (one leading forward, one aft)
15.   Lower stunsail boom
16.   Sheet
17.   Guys (one leading forward, one aft)
18.   Guy

I6/2   **The rigging of the topmast studding sail**
1.   Halyard block
2.   Halyard
3.   Topmast stunsail yard
4.   Thimble for downhauler
5.   Downhauler
6.   Topmast stunsail
7.   Downhauler block
8.   Sheet block
9.   Main stunsail boom
10.   Topmast stunsail sheet
11.   Fall of the downhauler
12.   Tack (leading forward)
13.   Sheet
14.   Fall of the sheet
15.   Main mast
16.   Main yard
17.   Main topmast
18.   Main topsail
19.   Main topsail yard
20.   Main topgallant mast

I6/3   **The fitting of the lower studding sail boom**
1.   Channel knee
2.   Main channel
3.   Eyeplate
4.   Hook or gooseneck
5.   Ferrule
6.   Boom
7.   Chain plate slot

I6/2

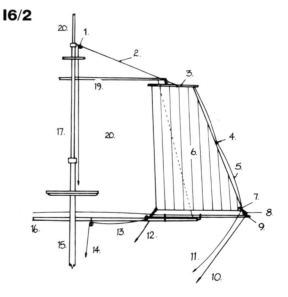

I6/1

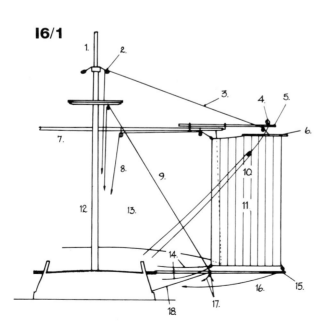

I6/3

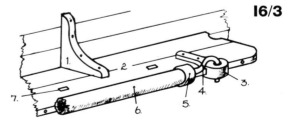

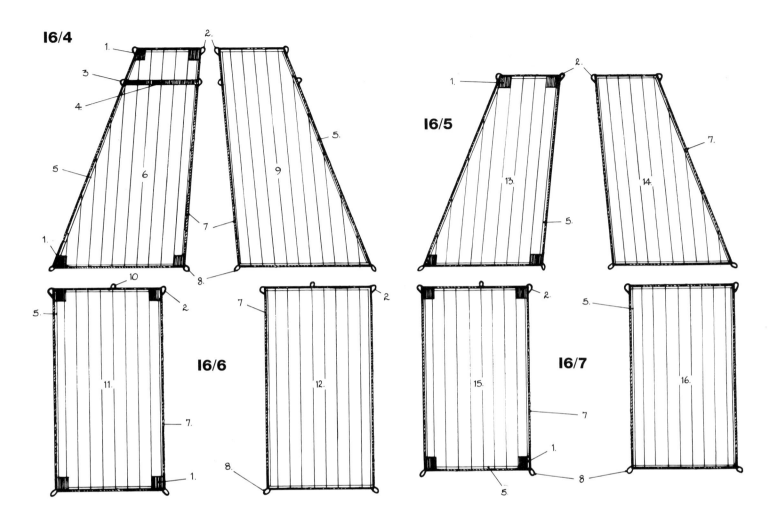

I6/4

I6/5

I6/6

I6/7

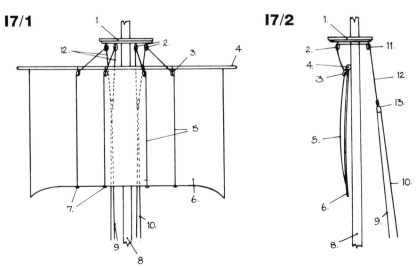

I6/4	**Main topmast studding sail**	
I6/5	**Fore topmast studding sail**	
I6/6	**Main lower studding sail**	
I6/7	**Fore lower studding sail**	
1.	Lining	
2.	Earings	
3.	Reef cringle	
4.	Reef band lining	
5.	Seam	
6.	Fore side of main topmast stunsail	
7.	Bolt ropes	
8.	Clews	
9.	After side of main topmast stunsail	
10.	Halyard cringle	
11.	Fore side of main lower stunsail	
12.	After side of main lower stunsail	
13.	Fore side of fore topmast stunsail	
14.	After side of fore topmast stunsail	
15.	Fore side of fore lower stunsail	
16.	After side of fore lower stunsail	

I7   BUNTLINES (no scale)

The fore course was rigged in the same manner whereas all of the topsails and topgallant sails were rigged with only two buntlines instead of four. The blocks for these sails were rigged on pendants fastened to their respective mastheads.

I7/1   View from forward

I7/2   View from side
1. Main top
2. Single sheave blocks
3. Buntline blocks
4. Main yard
5. Buntlines
6. Main course
7. Buntline cringles
8. Main mast
9. Fall of the buntline tackle
10. Standing part of the buntline tackle
11. Single sheave block
12. Fall of the buntline
13. Double block

I Sails

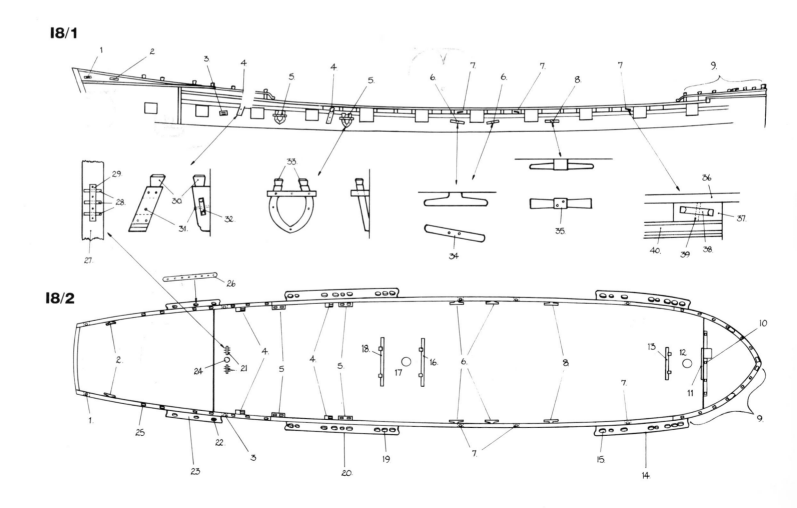

I8/1

I8/2

19 VARIETIES OF BLOCK (1/16 scale)

1. Common single-sheaved block, side elevation
2. Common single-sheaved block, end elevation
3. Double-sheaved block (type used for the jeers)
4. Treble-sheaved block (type used for the catblock)
5. Sister block
6. Long tackle block
7. Sheet block
8. Spritsail sheet block
9. Shoulder block (type used for clewlines)
10. Deadeye with concave groove for shrouds
11. Deadeye with flat groove for chain plates
12. Shoe block (used for buntline falls)
13. Lignum vitae sheave
14. Sheave pin
15. Score for pendant rope

19

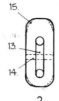
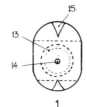

1.　　　　2.　　　　3.　　　　4.

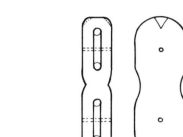
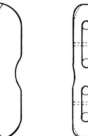
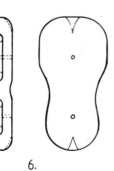

5.　　　　6.

7.　　　　8.

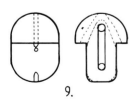

9.　　　10.　　11.　　　　12.

J   Boats

J1/3   Elevation and section
1.   Transom
2.   Stern post
3.   Keel
4.   Stringer supporting the thwarts
5.   Thwarts
6.   Stem post
7.   Rabbet of the stem post
8.   Rabbet of the keel
9.   Tiller
10.   Stern sheets
11.   Sheer strake
12.   Knees
13.   Pillars supporting the thwarts
14.   Gunwale
15.   Breast hook
16.   Oar, 15ft 3in
17.   Oar blade
18.   Shaft
19.   Loom
20.   Handle
21.   Frame
22.   Bottom boards
23.   Keelson
24.   Stringer

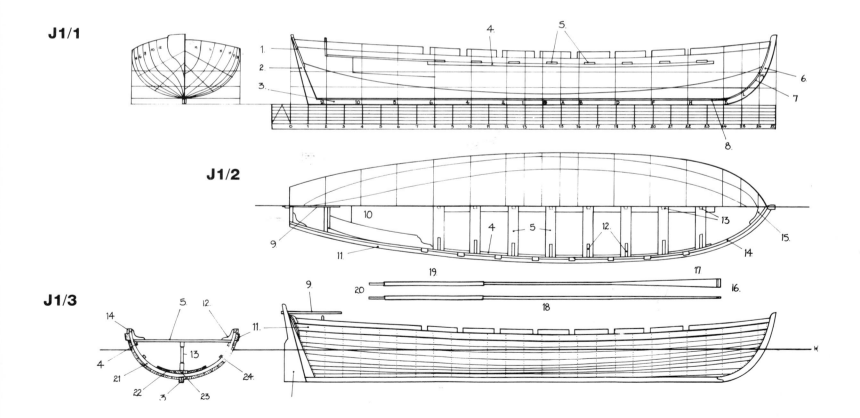

J1/1

J1/2

J1/3

J2 **YAWL,** *c*1715 (1/64 scale)
Length 17ft
Breadth 5ft
Depth 2ft

J2/1 **Lines and arrangement**

J2/2 **Plan and waterlines**

J2/3 **Elevation and section**

J2/4 **Bow view showing anchor transportation**
1. Gunwale
2. Stringer supporting the thwarts
3. Thwarts
4. Transom
5. Stem post
6. Stern post
7. Rabbet of the stem post
8. Keel
9. Rabbet of the keel
10. Trunk
11. Pawl ring
12. Pawl
13. Sternsheets
14. Windlass
15. Windlass retaining block
16. Knees
17. Gunwale
18. Thwarts
19. 14ft oar
20. Oar blade
21. Shaft
22. Loom
23. Handle
24. Stringers
25. Tiller
26. Sheer strake
27. Handspike for the windlass
28. Keel
29. Keelson
30. Bottom boards
31. Windlass cable entering trunk
32. After anchor painter
33. Anchor cable
34. Cable from windlass
35. Fore anchor painter
36. Strop around anchor palms
37. Crown of the anchor

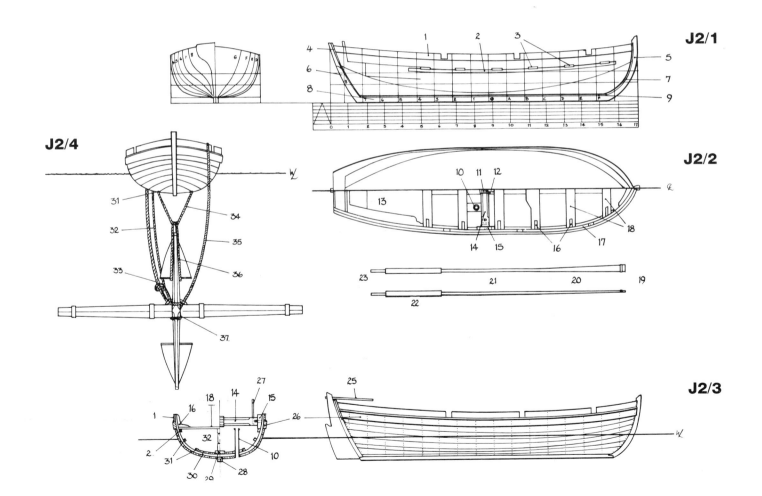